Pisces Guide to

CARIBBEAN
REEF ECOLOGY

Pisces Guide to

CARIBBEAN REEF ECOLOGY

William S. Alevizon

 Pisces Books™

Copyright © 1994 by Lonely Planet Publications
Head Office: PO Box 617, Hawthorn, Vic 3122, Australia
Branches: 150 Linden St, Oakland, CA 94607, USA
              10a Spring Place, London NW5 3BH, UK
              71 bis rue du Cardinal Lemoine, 75005 Paris, France

Library of Congress Cataloging-in-Publication Data
Alevizon, William S.
    Pisces guide to Caribbean reef ecology / by William
S. Alevizon.
        p.   cm.
    Includes bibliographical references and index.
    ISBN 1-55992-077-7
    1. Coral reef ecology—Caribbean Sea. 2. Coral reef
fauna—Caribbean Sea. 3. Fishes—Caribbean Sea. I.
Title. II. Title: Guide to Caribbean reef ecology.
QH109.A1A44 1993
597'.0526367'0916365—dc20   93-2430
                                             CIP

Printed in Hong Kong

CONTENTS

FOREWORD

With the development of technology and communications, dive training has become less expensive and diving trips more affordable. Throughout my career as a marine biologist and diver, I have witnessed the destruction of coral reefs as careless divers and boaters, uncontrolled development, lack of management, pollution, and overfishing turned what nature took millions of years to produce into piles of rubble. There is a desperate need to develop high-quality educational programs and materials to enhance public awareness of fragile ecosystems such as coral reefs. Publications such as this book, explaining the richness and fragility of coral reefs, should become as essential to divers as are tanks and fins.

Caribbean Reef Ecology will be enjoyed both by those interested in nature in general as well as by true coral reef aficionados. Dr. Alevizon, a scientist with extensive experience in Caribbean coral reefs and a restless fighter for their preservation, delights us with this work. Throughout the text, illustrations, and photographs, one can feel the greatness and beauty of coral reefs, and also learn a great deal about the ecology of some of the most conspicuous reef fishes of the region. At the same time, we are warned about common causes of reef destruction and advised on ways to lessen these threats by following some simple and basic codes of behavior.

Meant for all, *Caribbean Reef Ecology* not only makes enjoyable reading, but also leads to a greater understanding of the underwater world and why it is worth preserving. I hope you agree with me that this and future generations should strive to keep the sea and its creatures as elements of inspiration rather than passing references in the careless history of man.

Vicente Santiago-Fandiño, Ph.D.
Caribbean Environment Program
United Nations Environmental Program
Kingston, Jamaica

PREFACE

This is a story of sorts about Caribbean coral reefs. I made my first foray into this magical world almost twenty years ago, and I still vividly recall the first shock of the sudden transition from the familiar world of sun and sky to the surrealistic visions lying so unsuspectingly just beneath the waves. That sense of wonder remains undiminished today. The ever-growing popularity of reef diving attests to the fact that I am by no means alone in this obsession. And that brings us to the reason for this book—to enhance the experience of reef watching by presenting an ecological perspective on the coral reef drama and its "cast of thousands."

This is only one of many stories that might be told about life on a coral reef, for the subject is far too vast to be properly treated in a single book or by a single author. This book is *not* a field identification manual. Such manuals have their value to be sure, but their very format tends to blur or conceal essential ecological relationships. What would *Hamlet* be if only one character at a time was allowed on stage? An ecosystem is much more than a collection of different species assembled in a common environment. It is a complex interplay of natural forces operating on an interconnected web of life against the backdrop of an ever-changing environment. People today want to know the *why's* and *how's* of the living world, not just the *who's*. Certainly, one of my aims is to provide an appreciation of some of the main characters of the reef story. But even more central is an attempt to integrate the roles and behaviors of the players with the "stage" and its various "sets," and the basic rules of this kind of "theater." In that sense, this is meant as a starting point for amateur reef ecologists.

It has been truly said that nothing in nature is random—there are good reasons that things are the way they are. If we fail to understand or perceive the logic in nature, the shortcoming is in us, not in the world. As chaotic as the world of the reef may appear, there is a reasonable explanation for all that we see, from the average size of sand grains to the color and shape of the tiniest fish. Discovering those reasons, or trying to, is one of the most rewarding activities imaginable. I have no idea why this is so; it just is for those of us so inclined. And I suspect that this same satisfaction may be found at all levels, from the novice underwater naturalist to the seasoned scientist.

It usually surprises sport divers to discover how little is really known about the hundreds upon hundreds of creatures that call the reef home, and the ways in which they interact with one another and their environment. Certainly we have made progress since the advent of scuba a few decades ago. But from the perspective of what is yet to be learned, we have just begun to scratch the surface. And so in a very real sense, all who explore the reef in the spirit of learning and understanding are pioneers. It is my wish that this book enhances that journey of discovery for all who choose to share in the adventure.

Bill Alevizon, Ph.D.
Gainesville, Florida

Pisces Guide to

CARIBBEAN REEF ECOLOGY

1

Caribbean Coral Reefs

WHAT IS A CORAL REEF?

A living coral reef is without question one of the most beautiful and fascinating natural environments on the planet. Anyone who has experienced this undersea wonderland first-hand will agree with this simple statement. The variety of life found here far surpasses anything else the sea has to offer. Many hundreds of different kinds of fishes, plants, and invertebrate animals may all be found on a single reef. Multi-hued coral colonies branch and billow in all directions. Sponges, sea fans, and other strange animals adorn the reef surface, providing even greater color and variety. And if this were not enough, a bewildering assortment of outlandishly colored fishes drift and dart through the surrounding turquoise waters above.

As we shall see, the term "coral reef" applies to a great variety of structures that occur in a great many places. Coral reefs are found in tropical seas throughout the world [Figure 1-1]. There are two large oceanic regions with extensive reef development, each with its own unique assemblages of corals, fishes, and other forms of reef life. The Indo-Pacific is an enormous area spanning southeast Asia through Polynesia and Australia, and far to the east across the Indian Ocean to Africa. This is by far the largest coral province, as well as the richest in terms of number of species. The other major

1

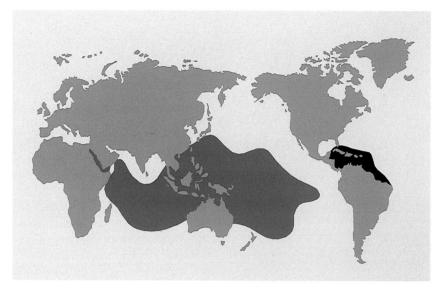

Figure 1-1. Coral reefs are found in three main regions of the world. The tropical western Atlantic [Caribbean] is shaded in black, while the Indo-Pacific and Red Sea are in dark grey. (Photo: Apollo Sports.)

region, and the subject of this book, is the tropical western Atlantic, which stretches from Bermuda in the north to Brazil in the south, and includes the entire Caribbean Sea. A third notable region, far smaller than these other two, is found in the waters of the Red Sea.

Coral reefs, huge though they may sometimes be, are primarily composed of individual animals called *polyps* that are quite small—few exceed the size of a pencil in diameter [Figure 1-2]. The polyps grow in groups called *colonies,* with each succeeding generation building its home upon the foundation of skeletons left by the last. The colonies in turn are typically attached to colonies of the same or other species, forming larger and more complex structures.

Coral reefs only grow in shallow tropical seas. A primary reason for this is their need for sunlight, for within the living tissue of the polyp are found tiny plant cells called *zooxanthellae.* These primitive algal cells provide coral with food, formed through the process of photosynthesis. In exchange, the plant cells receive nutrients and a place to live from their animal hosts. In truth then, corals are composite organisms, part animal and part plant. Each individual has what amounts to its own internal grocery store, and most of its nutritional needs are fulfilled in this way.

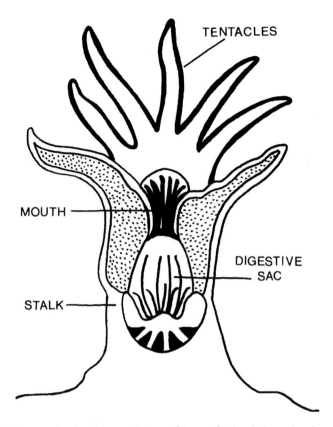

Figure 1-2. The coral polyp–tiny architect of the reef. The skeleton has been omitted to provide a view of polyp structure. (Illustration: Ruth Rasche.)

Coral polyps also regularly feed on small creatures floating by. These are captured by sticky stinging tentacles and passed to a simple digestive system. Usually, this type of feeding only occurs at night when the tempting tentacles are relatively safe from the searching eyes and mouths of hungry fish. During the day, feeding tentacles are withdrawn into the protection of a hard skeleton formed by the polyp from limestone extracted from seawater [Figure 1-3].

Over 50 species of reef-building corals are found in the western Atlantic region. Each forms colonies of characteristic shape, size, and color, although these are subject to some modification by local conditions.

Coral colonies exhibit three basic growth forms called *branching, massive,* and *plate-like* [Figure 1-4]. Becoming familiar with such colony traits makes the task of coral identification much easier. Some species, however, are highly similar and require closer scrutiny for proper identification. The reef-building polyps are not the only kind of corals; there are some that secrete flexible rather than stony skeletons. These are called *octocorals,* and they are a prominent feature of many Caribbean reefs.

Growing amid the coral colonies are certain kinds of algae that, like their animal associates, also form limestone skeletons. These may contribute substantially to the solid framework of the reef. Upon the rocky base built by the corals and algae grows an assortment of sponges and other animals and plants, giving the entire structure even greater complexity and variety, and completing the formation of the wondrous entity we call the coral reef.

a

Figure 1-3. A coral colony by day [a] and by night [b]. (Photo: Holly Hart.)

b

a

b

Figure 1-4. Three basic growth forms of coral colonies: branching (a), massive (b), and platelike (c). (Photos (a, c): Louisa Preston; Photo (b): W. Alevizon.)

c

THE STRUCTURE OF CARIBBEAN REEF ENVIRONMENTS

When we snorkel or scuba dive about coral reefs, we note distinct changes in their overall appearance. We may see solid coral carpets here, thick stands of seagrass there, and a mixture of small reefs and sand patches farther on. Such differences are the result of the interactions between seafloor characteristics, water movement, and light penetration on the biology of the different corals and other sea life. As the sea deepens and the shorelines of islands and continents give way to the open ocean, these factors often tend to vary in much the same way at many locations. This results in coastal environments of similar structure throughout the region. Understanding the fundamental structure of Caribbean coral reef environments is not difficult, and adds immeasurably to our understanding of the ecology of all reef life.

There are numerous ways to classify habitats within any environment. While such schemes are sometimes useful in studying and understanding an areas' ecology, remember that our subdivisions of the natural world are largely artificial, and a matter of human perspective. Features that people might use to distinguish and separate adjacent habitats often have little meaning to many of the animal residents of an area.

Most Caribbean reef environments consist of four different and adjacent kinds of areas or "zones" that exist as bands roughly paralleling the shoreline [Figures 1-5 and 1-6]. The width of these zones and the extent of the en-

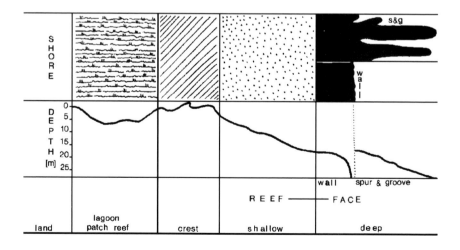

tire inshore ecosystem vary widely among different locations. In some areas, the shoreline gives way abruptly to sheer coral walls and water several thousand feet deep within a distance of a few hundred meters from shore. Elsewhere (the Florida Keys, for example) a shallow undersea shelf extends many miles out to sea.

In some cases, the boundaries between different zones are fairly sharp and abrupt. In others, zones grade gradually into one another. Sometimes, an entire zone may be missing. Nonetheless, with a bit of practice one may readily learn to recognize these different kinds of areas, and how they have been modified by local conditions.

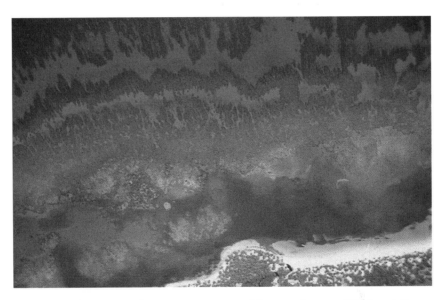

Figure 1-6. Aerial view of a representative Caribbean reef system. The beach [lower right] gives way to the lagoon with its dark seagrass beds. The reef crest is seen as an irregular rust-and-white band running parallel to the shore and separating the lagoon from the reef face—it is broken into fragments by frequent channels. Seaward of the crest is the upper reef face, here separated from the deeper lower face, with its prominent spur-and-groove formations, by a wide band of sand. (Photo: Erkki Siirila.)

◀ *Figure 1-5. A diagrammatic view of the structure of Caribbean reef environments. (Illustration: Ruth Rasche.)*

The Reef Crest

The best reference point on Caribbean reefs is the reef crest, a highly distinctive and easily identified area [Figure 1-7]. As the name suggests, this is the highest [shallowest] part of the reef, with some corals actually breaking the sea surface at low tide. The crest may be easily seen from the shore or the air as a brownish-orange band framed by a white line of breaking waves along its outer margin. It represents the dividing line between the shoreward lagoon and the seaward reef face. The crest stands like a massive wall, absorbing and dissipating the tremendous force of incoming waves. This is a structurally unstable area of the reef, as heavy storm waves regularly break off coral branches and tumble entire colonies about. It is also the least varied area in terms of corals, for a single species called elkhorn coral forms most of the reef here.

Figure 1-7. A snorkeler's view of the reef crest. (Photo: W. Alevizon.)

The Lagoon

Behind the crest lie the protected waters of the lagoon, offering welcome shelter to beleaguered sailors since people first took to the sea. This is the province of patch reefs, coral sand, seagrass, and mangroves. The lagoon is a marvelously rich habitat for some of the most heavily exploited animal life of the region, including spiny lobster, conch, fish, and sea turtles.

Patch reefs. Lagoonal patch reefs are isolated coral islands surrounded by seas of sand and grass [Figure 1-8]. They may be composed of few or many different kinds of corals, and they may be the size of a small car or larger than a football field. Most are intermediate between those extremes, perhaps averaging 20–70 meters in diameter, with a round to oval shape. The serene waters above the patch reefs of Caribbean lagoons are among the best places in the world for snorkeling, and for first becoming acquainted with reef life. Larger patch reefs are generally occupied by a rich assortment of fishes.

A notable feature of Caribbean patch reefs is a bare sand "halo" that surrounds the base of the reef for a distance of about 1–2 meters in all directions [Figure 1-8]. Some scientists have speculated that the halo is the result of grazing by plant-eating fishes and sea urchins. However, the halo is also sometimes present around reefs that have no such animals nearby. For

Figure 1-8. A diver marks the edge of the halo surrounding a patch reef in the Bahamas. (Photo: W. Alevizon.)

this reason, it seems probable that other forces are sometimes at work as well to create the effect. The halos are particularly evident from the air, and enable one to readily spot a dark patch reef amid equally dark seagrasses.

Seagrass. Seagrasses are a group of marine plants that form a distinctive habitat occupied by a characteristic community of other plants and animals [Figure 1-9]. Seagrass beds are most often found amid patch reefs in the calm waters of the lagoon. Compared with coral reefs or mangroves, seagrass is a structurally simple habitat, with little variety or physical complexity. There is scarce shelter here above the grass blades, save for the occasional sponge, octocoral, or small coral head. Animals active here by day are mainly small invertebrates and fishes that rely heavily on concealment—either through camouflage or burrowing. Even the formidably defended long-spined sea urchin restricts its feeding visits to seagrass beds to the hours of darkness. Except for a few "oddballs" like the well-armored sea turtle and trunkfish, seagrass is mostly a "night spot" for larger animals.

After sunset however, a variety of fishes venture forth and in the blackness find a measure of protection from the large and lethal predators that patrol this domain. Most of the fish that feed at night in the seagrass take shelter on the reef by day, and it is there that the nitrate-rich remains of their

Figure 1-9. Seagrass and its residents. (Photo: Louisa Preston.)

nocturnal foraging trips are eliminated. Through this process, and through predation on these night feeders by larger reef fishes, a link is established that directly transfers vital nutrients from the seagrass beds to the reef proper, and so promotes the growth of reef plants and corals.

Seagrass also serves as a home for countless juvenile reef fishes. While still small, these are able to use the limited shelter available in seagrass beds to good advantage. But continued growth makes them increasingly vulnerable to larger predators, and they must move or die. Many of these fish perish to predators in the seagrass, never reaching the reef to mature and reproduce. But a fortunate few successfully relocate to a home that offers shelter in the proper scale to their increasing size.

In a sense then, seagrass beds represent not only a prolific energy source regularly tapped by reef life, but also a large reservoir of ready recruits to nearby reefs—a "reserve army" of sorts. For these reasons, the health of seagrass areas is intimately related to the health and resiliency of nearby reef communities.

Mangroves. Where the waters of the lagoon give way to dry land, there frequently exists a transitional area, part sea and part shore. This is the world of the mangroves, a rather unique group of trees that is able to tolerate direct immersion in seawater. Mangroves line the shores of many tropical islands and coastlines, and contribute to the richness of reef life by providing both food and shelter to a variety of animals [Figure 1-10]. The un-

Figure 1-10. The world of the mangrove, seen from below the sea surface. (Photo: Doug Perrine.)

usual and complex root system forms a nursery ground for young reef fishes. Falling leaves and nesting birds add nutrients to the sea below, enhancing plant growth. True pioneers, mangroves play a key role in building land from the sea by trapping and consolidating sediments that would otherwise be swept away and dissipated.

The Reef Face

On the seaward side of the reef crest lie rapidly deepening waters and the reef face. This area extends from the seaward wall of the reef crest to the lower limits of reef growth. The reef face may be divided into two zones, upper and lower. The shallower upper reef face is characterized by gentle slopes, a very large number of coral species, and typically an abundance of staghorn coral [Figure 1-11]. This zone usually extends from about 3–20 meters in depth.

Figure 1-11. The shallow reef face is characterized by patches of staghorn coral. (Photo: W. Alevizon.)

The deep or lower reef face extends from the margin of the upper face into waters too poorly lit to permit coral growth. This zone is largely dominated by mountainous star coral, which forms high ridges or spurs, interspersed with sand channels or grooves [Figure 1-12]. Spur-and-groove formations run roughly perpendicular to shore, and disoriented divers may use this fact to find the way home. In some cases, the reef face may plunge abruptly and nearly vertically to great depths [Figure 1-13]. In these situations, differences in the character of the marine life observed on the horizontal and vertical faces of the reef, only a few meters apart, is truly noteworthy.

Figure 1-12. Spur and grooves of the deep reef face. (Photo: Paul Hart.)

Figure 1-13. The wall—another form of the deep reef face. (Photo: Paul Hart.)

Hardgrounds

In addition to the kinds of living coral reefs previously described, Caribbean coastal environments often contain a second type of reef habitat. This is called hardgrounds or live bottom. It consists of a low platform of limestone covered with a living carpet of sponges, octocorals, and encrusting plants and animals [Figure 1-14], but containing few live reef-building coral colonies.

Figure 1-14. Hardgrounds are rich in sponges, octocorals, and fishes.
(Photo: John Halas.)

Rising only a meter or so from a sandy seafloor, hardgrounds are the erod-ed bases of ancient coral reefs that have been worn down by the forces of nature until little remains. The hard substrate is perforated like a giant sponge by numerous cavities, holes, and crevices that give shelter to a multitude of animals. The platform also provides fine attachment sites for octocorals and sponges, and the long-dead reef is thereby transformed into a fairy garden, alive with waving sea fans and colorful reef fishes.

Hardgrounds may occur as scattered mounds among the patch reefs of the lagoon, or as large terraces in deeper water. They provide added diver-sity to the coral reef environment, and are a great place to explore in their own right. Hardgrounds are a true reef-type habitat; others such as seagrass, sand, and mangroves will be referred to later as off-reef habitats.

THE ECOSYSTEM PERSPECTIVE

The description of Caribbean reef environments presented here is at the broadest of scales. In practice, many ecologists might further subdivide certain of these zones and habitats, perhaps distinguishing between several types of seagrass habitats, or recognizing several distinct parts of the reef crest. Regardless of the scheme or its purpose, you are reminded that such lines are in fact drawn more for human convenience than as a reflection of the real world. Nature does not partition herself with hard and fast boundaries, and that simple fact is one of the greatest challenges in understanding the ecology of complex ecosystems such as coral reefs.

We have seen in this chapter that the coral reef environment is composed of an intricate mixture of different, yet interrelated places occupied and shared by a wide variety of living things. To understand the ecology of the most humble reef creature, one must always remember that a coral reef is not an island unto itself, but rather one component of an integrated tropical ecosystem that includes many other distinct kinds of areas. The creatures and resources of these interact in many ways with reef life, and they are an essential part of reef ecology.

2

CORAL REEF ECOLOGY

THE VOCABULARY OF CORAL REEF ECOLOGY

Every science has its own unique vocabulary, and ecology is no exception. Before launching an exploration of reef ecology, let us review some essential terms and concepts. The obvious place to begin is with the term "ecology" itself. The word is often misused in popular literature, frequently being incorrectly equated with "environment," or loosely identified with such activities as removing beer bottles from the roadside. But ecology is neither of these things. It is simply that branch of biology that deals with the *distribution* and *abundance* of living things. Distribution in this sense refers to where organisms are (or are not) found, while abundance refers to how many occur in different places. In most cases, patterns of both distribution and abundance are the result of complex interactions between many factors. Thus, there are seldom simple answers to such seemingly simple questions as, "Why are there so many fish here?"

The living world may be viewed from a wide range of perspectives, ranging from the microcosm of atoms and molecules to the macrocosm of the biosphere—the planetary shell of life. And in between are a host of intermediate levels. Ecologists primarily deal with life at three levels of organization. The most basic of these is the *population,* a term used to refer to a particular group of individuals of the same species—all of the people in New York City, or all the spiny lobsters on Palancar Reef. More complex

for obvious reasons is the *community,* consisting of all the populations oc-
cupying a particular place—all of the living things on Palancar Reef. Finally,
the term *ecosystem* is used to refer to a biological community along with
the non-living parts of its environment—all of the living creatures of Palancar Reef along with the surrounding rocks, sediments, water, and all that these
contain. Our comparative understanding of these levels is related to their complexity—we know a good deal more about how populations function than
we do about the workings of ecosystems.

THE FLOW OF NUTRIENTS AND ENERGY

Two chains—major pathways of energy and nutrient movement through
ecosystems—are commonly distinguished by ecologists. These are differ-
entiated on the basis of their inputs. The *grazing chain* begins with the con-
version by plants of the energy contained in sunlight, and follows the fate
of this energy as it moves through various levels of consumers of living tissue. In contrast, the *detrital chain* deals with the disposition of the decom-
posing fragments of once-living creatures.

Such an approach greatly simplifies analysis of the ways in which energy and nutrients move through the system, for these vital quantities may flow
through many thousands of individual links (species) in complex communities such as coral reefs. Both routes are really part of a single integrated
process, but there are good reasons for considering them separately. In
each case, the major "players" tend to be quite different kinds of organisms.
Additionally, in some cases (including the oceans), the two processes show
a degree of physical separation. Except for shallow coastal waters, most
oceanic "grazing" occurs in the water column, whereas the breakdown of
detritus is usually concentrated on or within the sea floor. We will now briefly
examine each of these pathways.

The Grazing Chain

To gain an overall appreciation for the organization of the grazing chain,
ecologists traditionally group community members into a relatively few distinct categories called *trophic levels.* The basis of this scheme is the primary
mode of nutrition. For example, all of the many animals of the reef that feed
on plants are considered together as a single group—the herbivores.

The number of trophic levels recognized varies with the ecosystem under
study. The grazing chain on coral reefs may best be understood in terms of

three main levels, respectively called *primary producers, primary consumers,* and *secondary consumers.*

Level One: The Primary Producers. This is the lowest trophic level. It forms the energy-nutrient base upon which all higher levels depend. This category consists nearly exclusively of those organisms capable of performing the magic we call *photosynthesis*—using the energy contained in sunlight to convert a few simple substances into new living tissue. These are, of course, the plants.

Level Two: The Primary Consumers. The second trophic level consists of community members that feed directly on living plants, converting some of that material into new animal tissue. Such animals are called *herbivores,* and a variety of fishes and invertebrates fill this particular role on coral reefs. In most ecosystems it is these resident herbivores alone that channel nutrients and energy from living plants to the animal kingdom. But corals, themselves part plant and part animal, have an internal exchange of nutrients and energy between the two parts. Thus, within the reef ecosystem there is a second major link between the two worlds.

Level Three: The Secondary Consumers. The third trophic level consists of the *carnivores;* those animals that kill and eat other living animals. Most reef fishes, all corals, and a variety of other invertebrate animals fall into this category. On coral reefs, carnivores represent a much richer group in terms of sheer numbers as well as variety than do the carnivores of most other ecosystems. A major reason for this is undoubtedly the correspondingly rich and varied supply of animal prey present on and around coral reefs. Along with the bountiful collection of resident invertebrates and fishes, there is also the zooplankton, a food source that we will now consider in its own right.

The Role of the Plankton

Ecosystems must not be considered complete and separate worlds unto themselves. All of the earth's ecosystems, from the deep sea trenches to the highest mountain forests, are ultimately tied together into a single planetary system of interactive matter and energy. As might be expected, a given ecosystem is generally most affected by its immediate neighbors. It follows then that one key to unravelling some of the mysteries of coral reef ecosystems is understanding the character of water movement about the reef, for in most cases this water has just recently been part of a very different world—that of the open sea.

Water movement varies not only among different sites on the same reef, but also often change seasonally and even daily at the same site. With changes in water movement, all sorts of other things may change as well: clarity, temperature, salinity, sediment levels, and most notably from the standpoint of hungry reef life, the kinds and amounts of living things suspended in the water column.

Along with a wide assortment of chemical substances, seawater contains a truly amazing group of microscopic animals and plants. By definition, all creatures that move passively at the mercy of winds and currents are termed *plankton*—the vagabonds of the sea. A few of the larger jellyfish may reach a size of a foot or more in diameter, and trail tentacles many feet in length [Figure 2-1]. But the vast majority of planktonic creatures are very

Figure 2-1. Jellyfish are among the largest of plankton. (Photo: Graham Teague.)

small; too tiny to be seen by the unaided eye. Some spend their entire lives in this wandering way, while others drift only for a while. The latter include the eggs and larval stages of most familiar reef life, including fish, crabs, and sea urchins. The water reaching coral reefs may be rich in such bounty. In these cases, plankton will represent a major input of food for reef life, as well as a source of new residents.

Most of the *zooplankton* (animal plankton) are themselves herbivores, feeding on the even tinier drifting plants of the open sea, called *phytoplankton.* In terms of reef ecology, zooplankters differ from reef-resident plant eaters in one essential way; they have accumulated most of their nutrients and energy in a distant, different ecosystem. Thus, rather than using or competing for resources within the reef community, they effectively reduce the community's dependence on *local* primary production. The overall energetic contribution of the plankton to the coral community is difficult to measure, and estimates vary. It is undoubtedly substantial, for reef planktivores are efficient, removing as much as 60% of the drifting animals from the passing water. Some plankton feeders are also known to capture and digest minute drifting plants—the phytoplankton itself. At present we know relatively little about the significance of this process on reef community nutrition.

The Detrital Chain

Have you ever wondered why the earth is not covered with a thick layer of dead plants and animals? Probably not while you were enjoying dinner, but that question may have crossed your mind at some other time. Well, one reason of course is that all communities include some animals that are voracious scavengers. These roam about in search of recently deceased animals to devour. Many sharks do this, in addition to feeding on live prey.

Another more easily overlooked reason is that there is also present in all ecosystems an amazing assortment of inconspicuous, often microscopic, organisms that work tirelessly to break down the dead tissues of other creatures. Most of the fruits of this labor are used by these decomposers for their own growth and metabolism. But there is something left over, and vital nutrients are thereby released back into the general environment. There, they are quickly taken up by plants and used for new growth. This endless pattern of nutrient cycling is an essential part of ecosystem function.

Some common reef invertebrates make a living by feeding directly on detritus. Much of this material is well-mixed with the comparatively energy-poor sediments of the seafloor, and animals feeding in this way must process a relatively large volume of material to extract sufficient energy.

Detritivores constitute a relatively minor component of the resident fauna of coral reefs, and the detrital chain plays perhaps somewhat less a unique role in this community than it does in most others. In part, this is because the corals themselves internally recycle nutrients through exchange between their plant and animal components, reducing the community's need for detrital processes.

A Perspective on Reef Energetics

One of the most pervasive and fundamental traits of all ecosystems is a predictable pattern to the amount of living matter contained in each of the trophic levels of the grazing chain. The amount invariably decreases dramatically as we move from the lower (primary) to the higher (tertiary) levels. Thus, the western prairies of America contain much more plant tissue than cattle tissue, and the cattle (if the ranchers allowed it) would support an even lower biomass of wolves and other predators.

But let our eyes wander about the "seascape" of the coral reef for a few moments. Where are the plants that are supposed to feed all the animals? To understand this apparent paradox, it is first necessary to appreciate a simple fact—fewer *rapidly growing* plants may produce more new food in a given period of time than a greater number of slower growing plants. Coral reefs are classic illustrations of this principle, achieving high production rates with low standing crops (biomass).

But this is only part of the answer. With the exception of the seaweeds, most of the plant life that supports coral reef ecosystems is not readily apparent. Microscopic algae grows on a host of surfaces on and around the reef, but is simply too small to be seen. Zooxanthellae, the tiny algal partners of the corals, are well-hidden within the polyps' tissue. Many Caribbean reef areas receive substantial nutritional support from nearby seagrass production, because many reef fishes feed directly on this source, or on herbivores that do. And finally, there is the plankton, transferring energy and nutrients from distant parts of the open ocean directly to the reef.

It is the sum of the production of new living tissue by all these sources that provides the energy and nutrients required to support all those reef animals. Although far less spectacular than the verdant foliage of the rain forest or the rolling grasses of the western prairies, the coral reef nonetheless also has its necessary pastures.

A final point worth emphasizing is that among all common reef animals, only the amazing corals themselves have the remarkable ability to directly use the two available energy input sources of the coral reef grazing chain—sunlight and plankton. This nutritional feat is without question one major reason that corals are able to form the basis for such an incredibly rich and productive ecosystem in the midst of waters so stripped of nutrients that they are often referred to as biological deserts.

THE CAST: MAJOR CATEGORIES OF REEF LIFE

One of the most notable characteristics of coral reefs is the rich assortment of living things found there, a diversity of life unmatched anywhere else in the sea. Here, we will very briefly introduce some of the main groups of characters that dominate coral reef communities. Fishes are mentioned here only in passing, as they are discussed in depth in later chapters.

Plants

Marine plants common on and around coral reefs fall into one of two major groups: algae and seagrasses. Algae may be attached to the seafloor (benthic), or drifting (planktonic). Benthic algae on coral reefs includes large (macroscopic) and tiny (microscopic) types.

Large benthic algae are commonly called seaweeds and are classified into three main types—green, brown, and red [Figure 2-2]. The characteristic color of the groups is determined by their photosynthetic pigments, colorful com-

Figure 2-2. A drifting brown seaweed provides refuge and transport for an entire community. (Photo: Graham Teague.)

pounds used by the plants to capture the energy of sunlight. Although sunlight appears white to our eyes, it is really composed of a spectrum of color, ranging from the infrared to the ultraviolet wavelengths. When sunlight penetrates the sea surface, the shorter red wavelengths are extinguished quickly. At depth, only the longer green and blue wavelengths remain. This is why everything underwater (even blood!) takes on these cooler hues.

The evolutionary result of these processes are the different colors of marine algae. Each contains pigments specialized to best use sunlight at different depths. Green algae (red-absorbing) are most common in intertidal areas and shallow water. In contrast, red algae (blue-absorbing) may be found hundreds of feet deep in the clear tropical waters typical of coral reef environments. Brown algae (yellow-green absorbing) are most commonly found at intermediate depths. These are general distribution patterns, and it is not unusual to find representatives of all three types together on shallow reefs. In addition to the macroscopic algae, a variety of microscopic forms are found on coral substrates and on the surfaces of the surrounding sand and seagrass. Unobtrusive as these tiny cells may be, we have seen that they play a major role in reef energetics.

The seagrasses are exclusively macroscopic plants. Unlike the algae, which evolved and remained for the most part in water, seagrasses are descendants of familiar land plants. They are capable of rapid growth and high rates of food production in the shallow transparent seas of the Caribbean. Seagrasses do not grow on the reef itself, but are found nearby in the sheltered waters of the lagoon.

In summary, both groups—algae and seagrasses—are integral parts of Caribbean reef ecosystems. First and foremost, of course, is the role they play in creating new living matter through the process of photosynthesis. Thus, they are a primary source of many biological compounds upon which all other reef life ultimately depends.

Invertebrate Animals

Because most people are much more familiar with large common animals of the land, it is quite easy to overlook the fact that by far most of the animals in the sea are invertebrates. Of the 26 or so major divisions (phyla) zoologists recognize within the animal kingdom, only *1* contains all the animals with backbones—the fishes, mammals, birds, reptiles, and amphibians. The other 25 are exclusively composed of invertebrates.

It would take many volumes to even begin to describe the amazing variety of form, life histories, behavior, and ecology of those invertebrate animals that inhabit coral reefs. In addition to feeding relationships, these creatures interact with one another and with fishes in a host of meaningful ways. Some infest the bodies of other animals as both internal and external parasites, and may be vectors for disease. Others engage in activities, such as burrowing or tunneling, that shape the very nature of the reef environment. Still others play a pivotal role in the health of reef life, removing parasites and damaged tissue from comrades. We still have a great deal to learn about these processes, and their effects on reef ecology. Six categories of invertebrates are particularly well-represented on coral reefs.

Cnidarians. This group contains the reef-building corals discussed earlier, as well as the closely related octocorals and sea anemones. The latter are common reef creatures that often associate closely with other kinds of animals. Tiny shrimp often find a safe home among the stinging tentacles used by the anemone to capture food [Figure 2-3].

Octocorals are extremely abundant in many reef habitats. These highly branched plankton-feeders are often mistaken for plants. Also commonly

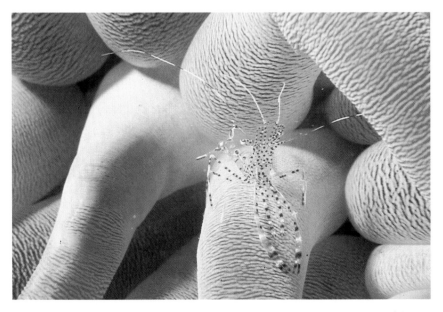

Figure 2-3. A cleaner shrimp finds a welcome home among the tentacles of the sea anemone. (Photo: Holly Hart.)

called gorgonians, they are a major structural component of Caribbean reef environments, adding both physical and biological diversity [Figure 2-4].

Sponges. The sponges are a colorful group of animals that are a familiar part of Caribbean reef seascapes [Figure 2-5]. They may be quite large, and some are able to easily contain a scuba diver with full gear in the central cavity. Sponges feed by creating currents that draw in seawater through thousands of tiny pores. This water is then filtered to remove microscopic life like bacteria as well as other plankton. The cavities of

Figure 2-4. An octocoral thrives in the clean waters of the reef face. (Photo: Graham Teague.)

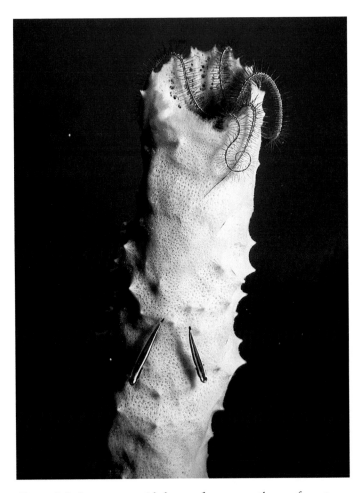

Figure 2-5. Sponges provide homes for many other reef creatures. (Photo: Graham Teague.)

sponges form a safe haven for a variety of fishes as well as invertebrates. Seemingly passive creatures, sponges nonetheless occasionally harm living corals. Some sponges use "chemical warfare" to bore their way into coral heads, thereby creating their own living space, a process that may eventually lead to the death of entire coral colonies.

Polychaetes. No one diving on Caribbean reefs fails to notice the common "featherdusters" and so-called "Christmas trees" that poke from tubes concealed within the reef substrate [Figure 2-6]. The bright extended feeding tentacles are instantly withdrawn if a possible enemy approaches too closely, causing these animals to seem to disappear before one's very eyes. These are sedentary members of a group called the *polychaetes,* an advanced and active group of worms. Sedentary forms are passive plankton feeders, but many of the mobile free-living forms are voracious predators, sometimes on corals. Certain of these (the fireworms) should be avoided by reef divers, as they are capable of inflicting a painful injury if touched. Polychaetes are much more numerous than a quick look might reveal, and form a major food source for some reef fishes.

Echinoderms. The spiny-skinned animals, or echinoderms, include a variety of familiar reef creatures that one would not think of as close relatives. Large sea stars (starfish) inhabit sand and seagrass areas around reefs, where they prey on buried mollusks. The smaller spindly-legged brittle stars

Figure 2-6. A featherduster with tentacle extended to catch plankton. (Photo: Holly Hart.)

[Figure 2-7a] are just about everywhere, with about 20 species common in Caribbean reef areas. These are mainly nocturnal predators that remain sheltered by day, often buried in bottom sediments or within the cavities of sponges. They feed in a variety of ways, as scavengers, predators, and on detritus. Brittle stars themselves are a delicacy for many reef fishes.

Sea cucumbers are odd creatures that feed mainly on the detritus mixed in the sediments of the sea floor, processing enormous quantities through their tubular bodies. They are common in off-reef habitats of sand and seagrass. Sea lilies, or crinoids, are delicately structured planktivores that become most common in the deeper water of the reef face [Figure 2-7b]. And finally, the familiar sea urchins are active herbivores, common in all reef environments [Figure 2-7c]. Some live in seagrass, while others shelter in crevices on the reef by day, emerging to actively forage on surrounding vegetation by night. During the last decade, a widespread and devastating plague of unknown origin took a heavy toll on the long-spined sea urchin, one of the Caribbean's best-known reef residents. In many locations, this species now seems to be making a strong comeback. Whether such events are part of regular long-term cycles or patterns, or simply responses to unusual events or conditions is unknown.

Figure 2-7. Reef echinoderms include the brittle star (a), crinoid (b), and sea urchin (c). (Photo (a): Paul Hart; Photos (b, c): Holly Hart.)

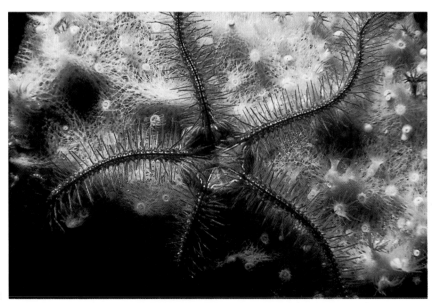

a

b

Figure 2-7. Continued.

c

Mollusks. The mollusks are a common and varied group of marine animals, with many species and different ways of life. Three groups are of particular interest here. The snails and their relatives are residents both of the reef as well as of seagrass and sand. These are slow-moving grazers, and many are herbivores. The highly-prized conchs, now badly over-fished throughout the Caribbean, belong to this group. Another notable member is the common flamingo tongue, a small brightly spotted carnivorous snail that may often be found grazing on sea fan polyps [Figure 2-8a]. Clams and scallops depend upon concealment and the heavy shell to keep predators at bay, but nonetheless they are heavily hunted by reef fishes and sea stars [Figure 2-8b]. These are active filter feeders, pumping water through strainers to remove food. Finally, there are the highly evolved predatory members of the group—the squids and octopi. These have well-developed nervous systems, complete with relatively large brains and eyes very much like our own. They are masters of color change, often so well camouflaged as to be virtually invisible even at close range. Octopi are benthic creatures, while the squid is an open-water hunter that feeds on a variety of large prey, including fishes [Figure 2-8c].

Figure 2-8. The flamingo tongue (a), scallop (b), and squid (c) are all familiar mollusks of reef areas. (Photo (a): Holly Hart; Photo (b): Paul Hart; Photo (c): Graham Teague.)

a

b

c

Figure 2-8. Continued.

Crustaceans. The final group we will mention here are the crustaceans—shrimps, crabs, lobsters, etc. [Figure 2-9]. These play a host of different roles in the life of the reef community. Some are scavengers, cleansing the reef of decaying animal remains. Some are active predators, and others omnivores. Many shrimp are "cleaners," gaining food by removing parasites from fish or invertebrates. Because of these benefits, the grateful host grants them a special "protected" status. Even when cleaning the mouths and teeth of the fearsome barracuda, they are allowed to go about their business without becoming a meal themselves. The spiny lobster, perhaps the premier delicacy of the Caribbean, is not a true reef resident but rather an occasional short-term visitor. Nonetheless, at times its numbers in reef areas are substantial. With high commercial value and ever-increasing fishing pressure however, the days of lobster-packed reefs would appear to be numbered.

a

Figure 2-9. Common reef crustaceans include the crab (a), spiny lobster (b), and countless shrimp (c). (Photo (a): Graham Teague; Photos (b, c): Paul Hart.)

b

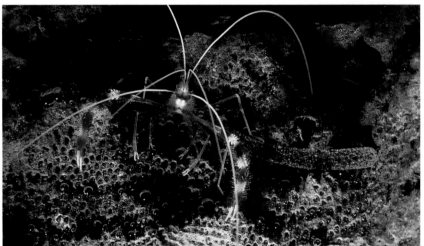

c

Figure 2-9. Continued.

Vertebrate Animals

The dominant group of reef vertebrates are, of course, the fishes. Representatives of other groups are occasionally observed feeding and taking shelter on Caribbean reefs, but these are really visitors that spend most of their time elsewhere. Typically, this includes sea turtles, which come to reef areas to feed on nearby plant life and occasionally rest in the protection afforded by the corals.

A few sea birds also will occasionally hunt around the reef; I was startled one day while diving in the Florida Keys to come face to face with a loon as I rounded a coral head! Observations of marine mammals such as dolphins and porpoises interacting with reef life are notably rare. It would seem that these creatures of the open sea have an aversion for approaching the reef proper. The only true vertebrate residents of Caribbean reefs are the fishes.

3

THE ECOLOGY OF REEF FISHES

CLASSIFICATION AND ANATOMY OF FISHES

Of all the creatures dwelling on coral reefs, none are more active or obvious than the fishes. It is safe to say that most divers spend a good deal more time fish watching than they do seeking out the smaller, well-hidden invertebrates of the reef. Perhaps more than any other single component of reef communities, fishes provide the best opportunity to observe essential features of reef ecology first-hand.

The term "fish" is not a formal category of biological classification, as is for example "bird," "amphibian," "reptile," or "mammal." We may loosely define a fish as an aquatic vertebrate that uses fins to swim and gills to breathe. Except for a few primitive jawless types, all living fishes belong to one of two main groups—that of the *sharks* (and their close cousins the rays), or a much larger group called the *bony fishes*. Fishes are the true masters of the ¾ of our planet that is covered by water, and live in almost every conceivable aquatic habitat. A fair number are freshwater residents, but most species are strictly creatures of the sea.

Bony fishes come in all shapes and sizes to be sure, but their basic body plan is fairly simple [Figure 3-1]. There are three main regions: the head, trunk, and tail. These are not sharply defined, but blend smoothly into one

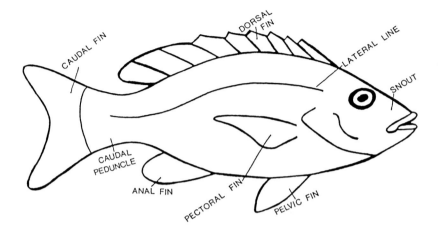

Figure 3-1. External anatomy of a bony fish. (Illustration: Ruth Rasche.)

another. For appendages, fish have a series of fins along the midline of both the upper (dorsal) and lower (ventral) surface of the body, and two sets of paired fins that correspond to our arms and legs—the pectoral and pelvic fins. The body terminates in the caudal fin, the main propulsive structure.

The fish body is covered and shielded by a strong but light external armor—the scales. These, along with the slimy mucous layer coating them, serve as protective barriers against mechanical injury and infection. Internally, the anatomy of the bony fish is remarkably similar to our own. With the exception of the use of gills rather than lungs as the main respiratory structures, the same major organs perform the same basic functions.

The sensory capabilities of fishes are well-developed. Fish eyes and ears are similar to our own, but adapted for sight and sound in water. Most reef fish are able to see color, many are capable of producing sound, and nearly all possess a sensory system not found at all in fully terrestrial vertebrates like ourselves. This is the lateral line system, a special kind of sound detector that enables fishes to sense nearby moving objects as well as stationary objects in their swimming paths. It is sometimes described as a "distant touch," allowing fish to navigate or to become aware of possible threats or prey without the need for vision.

A second unique adaptation of bony fishes is the swim bladder—an organ that permits them to maintain neutral buoyancy over a wide range of depths. I doubt there exists a diver who has not at one time or another looked with envy at the perfect balance of a hovering fish, unburdened by an array of diving equipment that merely allows us, for a few moments, to simulate what these creatures do so effortlessly.

In this book, we will see some of the marvelous ways in which basic fish design has been modified among reef fishes to provide an incredible diversity of form and function. Perhaps the most remarkable aspect of the body plan of bony fishes is its pliability, providing the group with almost limitless possibilities to adapt to a varied and changing environment.

GENERAL ADAPTATIONS OF REEF FISHES

Body Plan

Of all the aquatic habitats on the earth, the richest are those of shallow coastal seas. Kelp forests and coral reefs offer fishes an unparalleled abundance and diversity of resources. It is no surprise then that these places have become primarily the domain of the group considered the apex of fish evolution—the perch-like fishes (order Perciformes) and their descendants.

Perch-like fishes probably evolved in a reef-like environment, and so possess a basic body plan that is well-suited to coral reef existence, where a premium is placed on maneuverability rather than sheer speed. While the latter may be generally more desirable in open water, the capture of food or avoidance of enemies in complex habitats like coral reefs often requires rapid changes in direction. The kind of fish body most adept at such aquatic acrobatics is of course quite different from one designed for swiftness alone. In most reef fishes, the body is deep and laterally compressed [Figure 3-2]. The pectoral fins are high on the "shoulders," and the pelvic fins are positioned directly below. This arrangement yields superb swimming control.

The unmatched maneuvering ability of coral reef fishes must be observed first-hand to really be appreciated. Do not be misled by the less-than-spectacular movements most commonly displayed—most of the time, reef fish are just "strolling" about. It is when they are pursuing prey or rivals, or themselves being pursued, that they really show their stuff.

Coloration

A notable trait of coral reef fishes is the seemingly endless variety of flamboyant color patterns they bear. There are two primary functions of coloration in animals: to advertise, or to conceal the owner's presence. Also, there is at times a necessity for species to be able to recognize others of their own kind. From these relatively simple needs has sprung the virtual kaleidoscope of hues and patterns worn by coral reef fishes.

Concealment is the most common goal in animal coloration, and there are a wide variety of strategies used to achieve that end. Entire volumes have

Figure 3-2. The basic body plan of reef fishes is well illustrated by the angelfish. (Photo: Graham Teague.)

been written on this topic alone, so we will just mention a few general principles here. First and foremost, we must appreciate the fact that particular patterns are designed to conceal *only* in particular contexts. Typically this is when the fish is motionless in the kinds of places where it habitually either rests or hunts. No color pattern is very good at hiding a fish in motion, and those species that spend most of the day actively swimming tend to have uniform hues that correspond to their watery backdrop [Figure 3-3].

Seen out of the proper context, many of the color patterns of reef fishes might appear anything but concealing. Nonetheless, these same colors may function to make the fish nearly invisible in the proper situation. It is extremely common for divers in reef areas to "suddenly" notice a large motionless fish nearby, a fish that they should have seen earlier, but that caught their eye only after the perspective (distance, viewing angle, lighting, etc.) had changed as the diver moved about.

Bold contrasting patterns serve to destroy the outline of a fish, and so prevent recognition of its shape. The characteristic color pattern of the Nassau

Figure 3-3. Fish always in motion wear uniform hues. (Photo: Paul Hart.)

grouper is a perfect example. This fish commonly hunts from caves at the sandy base of the reef. It sports alternating very dark and light bands [Figure 3-4], with one of the colors matching the background, and the other contrasting. Thus, when seen against its places of ambush and rest, it is often difficult to pick out, despite its considerable size.

Some fish achieve concealment by wearing colors that accurately picture the hiding place itself. Scorpionfish are masters of this strategy, blending perfectly with the algal covered rocks upon which they rest [Figure 3-5]. Others actually disguise themselves as something else—the trumpetfish for example will take on the colors and behavior of a waving octocoral branch, aligning itself with the other branches and swaying with them in unison [Figure 3-6].

Some color patterns are intended to advertise the bearer's presence. This may be an advantage in warning others that an area is occupied, thereby reducing the need for physical conflict. Warning colors tend to be bold, saturated hues covering wide expanses of the body. The most frequent color combinations are for good reason also the most visible—the same colors that we use for warning signs on our roadways: red and black, yellow and black, or red and white. Some fish use even gaudier hues. Those of the fairy basslet [Figure 3-7] illustrate perfectly the essentials of warning coloration.

Feeding Structures

The structure of the mouth, teeth, and jaws vary greatly among reef fishes, and that should come as no surprise. Mouths designed for taking plankton would be expected to differ from those intended to bite off polyp tentacles, scrape algae, capture and swallow other fish, or grasp and crush shells [Figure 3-8]. As a group, coral reef fishes have adapted to successfully exploit the full gamut of food resources present in their environment.

Figure 3-4. The Nassau grouper is difficult to spot as it lurks motionless on the reef floor. (Photo: W. Alevizon.)

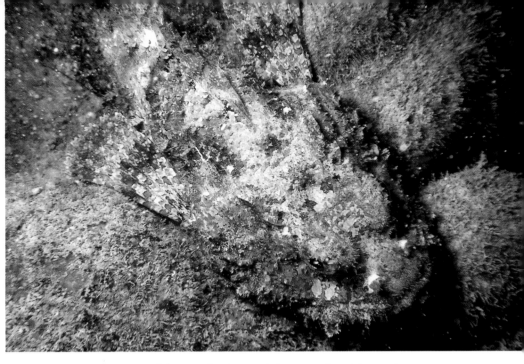

Figure 3-5. A scorpionfish waits for dinner. (Photo: Graham Teague.)

Figure 3-6. A trumpetfish hides among the branches of a gorgonian. (Photo: W. Alevizon.)

GENERAL ECOLOGY

Reproduction and Dispersal

Coral reef fishes are creatures of the tropics, a place where there is little to mark the passing of the seasons. Many reef fishes reproduce at regular intervals throughout the year, or at the least during several periods of the annual cycle. Many have distinct spawning peaks—periods of intensified reproductive activity. Frequently, these anticipate the best feeding opportunities for rapidly growing larvae. There is also mounting evidence that in some cases spawning is synchronized with predictable patterns of water movement, particularly with those that return offspring to the same reefs on which they were spawned.

Individual reef fishes produce many—sometimes hundreds of thousands—eggs with each spawning. In most cases the eggs are simply released into the plankton of the open sea, and left to their own devices. The plankton is a dangerous place for eggs and larvae. Only a lucky few survive long

Figure 3-7. Warning colors of the fairy basslet. (Photo: Graham Teague.)

a

Figure 3-8. Different food, different mouths. Butterflyfish (a) nips polyps, parrotfish (b) scrape algae, groupers (c) swallow fish whole, and porcupinefish (d) crush shells. (Photo (a): Graham Teague; Photo (b): Louisa Preston; Photo (c): Doug Perrine; Photo (d): Holly Hart.)

b

c

d

Figure 3-8. Continued.

enough to encounter a reef area in which to settle to the seafloor, and eventually take up new lives as reef fish.

We know relatively little about these early life stages. Fishes are tiny and transparent during larval life, and after settling are usually highly cryptic in both appearance and behavior. Do most reef fish remain much where they settle, to live or die wherever they happen to land? Or do they as a matter of course relocate to particular habitats as they grow, seeking larger and larger structures to provide food and shelter appropriate to their increasing size [Figure 3-9]? We do not yet know the answers to these crucial questions, although it is quite clear that they are a key elements of the coral reef story.

The Use of Space: Distribution and Abundance Patterns

One of the real rewards in learning to observe wildlife is gaining the experience to know where and how to look for particular species. The more familiar you become with reef environments, the more obvious it becomes that most reef fishes are not scattered about more or less randomly, but rather tend to be more common in certain kinds of places. In a similar manner, the more you travel to distant reef areas within the Caribbean region, the more apparent it is that there are often distinct differences in the overall composition of the fish assemblages at each; species that seem to be "everywhere" at one location may be missing or difficult to find at another. Particular groups may dominate reefs at one location, but constitute a relatively minor component at others.

We are still far from being able to convincingly explain the reasons for most of these differences, and this is the real business of reef fish ecology. Nonetheless, it is possible to make a few general statements regarding the types of factors that come into play. In this context, we distinguish between the kinds of things that most influence reef fish ecology at the *local* level (i.e., within the same reef system) as opposed to the *geographic* level (among distant reef systems), for these factors tend to be quite different.

At the local scale of reef zones and habitats, reef fishes tend to exhibit predictable distribution and abundance patterns. In most cases, these may be directly related to the nature of the resources (chiefly food and shelter) present in different kinds of areas. As an example, if we wish to observe the redlipped blenny, we will be most successful if we search partially eroded skyward-facing surfaces of shallow reefs. This is predictably as true in the Bahamas as it is in distant Honduras. Also, in both areas plankton feeders will invariably gather in swarms above promontories where currents are particularly favorable for feeding, and the shelter of reef is just below.

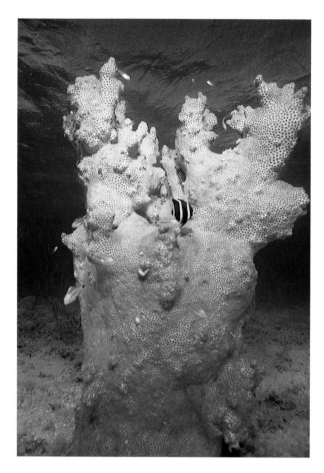

Figure 3-9. Juvenile reef fish often reside on sponges and gorgonians in off-reef habitats. (Photo: John Halas.)

At the geographic level however, larger scale climatological or oceano-graphic processes may limit distribution and/or abundance of species. Re-gardless of the supplies of food and shelter, some fishes may be poorly rep-resented in a given area if their planktonic larvae have a difficult time reaching it. Alternately, differences in things like water temperature may in-teract in subtle ways with a species' biology to allow it to be quite successful in some areas, but not in others. Thus, if we visit reefs of the Florida Keys, we will often encounter the blue angelfish. But we will not see this species in Honduras, search as we might. It is simply absent from the western and southern Caribbean. In a similar manner, the fairy basslet is common on both deep and shallow reefs throughout the Bahamas, but is not to be found in the Florida Keys, less than 70 miles away.

The fact that many reef fishes favor particular places does not by any means imply that they are restricted to those—they just are more common there. Reef fish, above all else, are opportunists—they will use whatever is available to the best of their ability, be it food or space. So we might note that with few exceptions, most common reef fishes occur to some degree in most or all of the reef habitats described earlier.

The Use of Food: Feeding Ecology

The abundance and variety of food resources available to fishes on coral reefs are probably good reasons why so many kinds of fishes are able to share the same environment. Some reef fishes are food specialists, adapted to use a few kinds of food very efficiently. In contrast, others are food generalists, with highly varied diets. Reef fishes in general are more adapted for feeding in a particular manner than on particular prey species. They hunt very broad categories of food types, such as plankton or other fishes, in certain kinds of places and at certain times of the day. Within this framework, they will eat pretty much whatever comes along, provided that they have the "equipment" to handle it.

Species differ of course in their abilities to capture and handle different types of prey. These differences are primarily due to variations in *feeding morphology*—the size and shape of the mouth, teeth, and jaws. Nonetheless, many reef fishes have quite generalized food habits, and a propensity for taking advantage of unusual food sources that may become present from time to time. Thus, the actual dietary composition of reef fish often reflects availability rather than preference, and so may vary markedly from day to day and from place to place.

Before discussing specific groups of feeders, let us compare some of the major differences between the two most fundamentally different kinds: those that use plants and those that use animals. A pervasive precept of biology is that among all living things, form follows function. Animals adapted mainly for eating plant material differ in predictable ways from their meat-eating relatives, particularly in terms of the main structures responsible for food processing: the teeth and digestive tract.

There are solid reasons for plant eaters to so differ from meat eaters. The basic unit of all life is the individual cell. While plant and animal cells share many similarities, there are also some fundamental differences. The two types of food therefore need to be processed differently. Plants are composed of cells with tough, strong protective walls made of cellulose, so eating plants

Figure 3-10. The teeth of a carnivore. (Photo: Graham Teague.)

requires greater initial mechanical breakdown and more extensive chemical processing than does the use of animal cells.

For this reason, herbivorous animals then tend to have large flat grinding teeth capable of physically crushing the tough cell walls, and a relatively lengthy digestive tract that allows for the slow digestion of plant cells. In contrast, meat-eaters tend to have sharp pointed or blade-like teeth, adapted for seizing and holding prey or for piercing and tearing [Figure 3-12]. They also tend to have a comparatively short digestive tract, because without cellulose walls animal cells may be digested more quickly. A quick look in your own mouth should assure you that humans are well equipped to process both plant and animal tissue, with cutting/piercing teeth in front (canines, incisors) and grinding/crushing teeth (molars) behind.

Not only does the anatomy of herbivores and carnivores differ; so does their feeding behavior. Plant tissue contains more water and less energy, ounce for ounce, than does animal tissue. The process of digestion of plant tissue is also less efficient. Thus, herbivores must spend a good deal more time feeding than meat-eaters to obtain the same amount of energy. It is not uncommon for plant eaters (reef fishes as well as herds of cows) to graze more or less continuously throughout the day. In contrast, many carnivores concentrate feeding activities within relatively short periods.

4

PLANT AND PLANKTON FEEDERS

INTRODUCTION

We will organize our discussion of reef fish ecology around the use of food resources, grouping species according to the *major* source of nutrition—plants, plankton, invertebrate animals, or fish. It must be emphasized that these categories are *not* necessarily mutually exclusive—many reef fishes regularly or occasionally feed upon several of these sources. Within each group, we will then look at alternate strategies used to exploit the opportunities presented by each kind of food resource. This chapter takes a look at fishes that feed on plants and those that feed on planktonic animals.

FISH THAT EAT PLANTS: THE HERBIVORES

The number of different kinds of Caribbean reef fishes that eat plants is low compared to the number of meat-eaters. Herbivores comprise only about 10% of all reef fish species in our area, and most belong to one of three families; the *parrotfishes, surgeonfishes,* and *damselfishes.* Herbivory may not be a particularly popular life-style among reef fishes, but it has some distinct advantages. Perhaps the most obvious is that the food source is widely available, and seldom if ever in short supply. As a result, reef herbivores do not need to spend much time or energy searching for food. The main disadvantage is that plant-eaters must feed more or less continuously throughout the day—a demand with consequences that may not be immediately obvious. Animals preoccupied with feeding are themselves vulnerable—much more likely to become meals than are animals hidden in protected shelters, or vigilantly watching for danger. Thus, like everything else, herbivory has its good and bad points.

Although there is not a particularly large number of different kinds of plant-eating fishes that dwell on Caribbean reefs, those present occur in sizeable numbers. Some, particularly parrotfishes, are also quite large. As one would expect, reef herbivores are most common in shallow well-lit waters where plants grow best. It has been "guess-timated" that on Caribbean reefs, plant-eaters tend to form the bulk of reef fish flesh at depths above thirty feet, while meat-eaters prevail at greater depths.

Anthropologists frequently contrast the life-style of people that live as no-madic hunters and gatherers with that of sedentary farmers. These two basi-cally different approaches to the problem of acquiring food also aptly distinguish the two main strategies employed by reef herbivores. Most are gatherers that roam the reef throughout the day, stopping frequently to graze. But some are sedentary, guarding and cultivating small patches of algae and spending most of their lives in a small area. We will look at both types of herbivores.

Nomadic Browsers

Parrotfishes. These are the largest and most colorful of the roaming reef herbivores [Figure 4-1]. The family name is derived from the brilliant hues and beak-like mouths that characterize the group. The cutting edge of the beak, which has replaced teeth in this group, is used to scrape and bite algae from the rocky coral surface. Their unusually powerful jaw muscles and strong set of inner teeth (called a pharyngeal mill) are used to pulverize coral into a fine powdery sand. The feeding process is noisy, producing rasping and crunching noises as the coral is scraped, bitten, and crushed. Nutrients are digested, and the remaining sandy wastes passed back out into the water. The sight of a parrotfish "dumping" small clouds of crushed coral as they swim is familiar to divers.

Because parrotfishes are large and numerous, a truly amazing amount of material is processed in this way over time. A single adult parrotfish may release more than a ton of sand every year. It follows then that a substan-tial amount of the fine sand found in coral reef areas is of such origin. Al-though you will not see the fact flaunted in travel promotions, it is proba-

Figure 4-1. Parrotfish are living coral processing plants. (Photo: Doug Perrine.)

bly safe to say that most of those lovely white Caribbean beaches are to a large extent composed of "fish poop"!

Why are parrotfishes considered herbivores if they eat coral? The answer is that most of the food found in their digestive systems is plant tissue. Still, there is no denying that parrotfishes also take in some animal tissue along with the plants. They may derive additional nutrition from the protective mucous coating covering living coral surfaces. Finally, parrotfishes will at times consume injured animals as well. So, it seems that parrotfishes are not strict vegetarians, but enough so to be considered herbivores.

Parrotfishes are inactive at night and are generally found wedged into holes and crevices in the reef, where they sleep until first light. Many species have the remarkable ability to secrete a mucous cocoon with which they cover themselves as they sleep. The cocoon presumably functions to mask the scent and skin texture, thereby reducing the likelihood of literally "being caught napping" by marauding predators of the night.

Despite their size and striking color patterns, parrotfishes are not always easy to identify. The reason for this is an unusually complex life cycle, in which individuals pass through several stages called *phases*. Even stranger is the fact that the passage from one stage to the next sometimes involves a functional sex change. Typically, all or most individuals are born as females. When these fish reach reproductive age, they are termed *intermediate phase* or *midphase* fish. These are usually drably colored, often in shades of grey or other muted hues [Figure 4-2a]. Some midphase fish eventually undergo a dramatic transformation to become large dominant breeding males, called *terminal phase* or more simply *termphase* fish. The transformation has been shown to be triggered by the release of hormones. Termphase individuals are typically brightly colored and frequently acquire a somewhat different body shape than their midphase counterparts [Figure 4-2b]. In most cases, they also grow to a greater size.

A consequence of all this is that parrotfish populations contain more females than males, an unusual condition among animal species. Additionally, most parrotfishes at times display aggressive territorial behavior, in which the termphase male maintains a jealous watch over a harem of females. Such aggression is usually directed only at other parrotfish. The advantages of this unusual life cycle are not at all clear, although judging by the success of the group there must be some.

The strikingly different appearances of the two phases caused a great deal of confusion when ichthyologists first began studying parrotfishes. Quite naturally, the midphase and termphase individuals of a particular species were considered members of two different species, and so there were at one time about twice as many kinds of parrotfishes believed to inhabit the reef.

Although many parrotfishes are brightly hued, some are quite cryptic both in color and habit. These are relatively small-bodied species that live in seagrass

a

b

Figure 4-2. Female (a) and male (b) stoplight parrotfish. (Photo (a): Louisa Preston; Photo (b): Doug Perrine.)

areas. They may be found by carefully searching near sponges, small corals, natural depressions, or any other feature offering a bit of shelter or concealment.

One particular member of the group, the midnight parrotfish, is unusual among the larger reef-roaming parrotfishes in that the coloration (deep blue with a few electric blue blotches) remains the same in sub-adults, midphase, and termphase. Perhaps this is related to their habit of forming mixed feeding aggregations with a surgeonfish (the blue tang) of similar hues. For schooling behavior to function effectively to deter predation, members of a given school should all look alike. Predators seem to be best able to subvert this particular defense when they detect an "oddball" within the school. So it may be no coincidence that the parrotfishes most often schooling with blue tangs is clad in matching colors, and that these do not change with age.

Surgeonfishes. These are the mid-sized models of Caribbean reef herbivores. They exemplify the basic reef-fish shape—deep-bodied and compressed. The family name stems from the sharp scalpel-like spine found on each side of the body near the base of the tail. This spine is retractable, and lies nearly flush with the tail when the fish is not threatened. When needed, it is a formidable weapon, and surgeonfishes rely on this as well as quickness and maneuverability to avoid predators. Surgeonfishes are commonly found feeding just about everywhere on and around reef areas by day.

The most common surgeonfish is the blue tang, a descriptive name only in the adult—juveniles are bright yellow. The blue tang appears to have two basic feeding modes: solitary and group [Figure 4-3]. Lone individuals are frequently found browsing about the reef, and this is the most common behavior. The group or schooling mode may be a method of overcoming the territorial defense of small damselfishes that would readily drive off a solitary individual. When feeding in the group mode, the school swims slowly over the reef a few feet above the coral. Suddenly, and for no discernable reason, an individual will quickly descend to feed, immediately followed by a number of its comrades. While hapless damselfish in the vicinity attempt to deal as well as possible with the nearest intruders, the horde quickly decimates the nearby stash of algae! Such feeding bursts generally last perhaps 15–20 seconds, and then the school moves on to repeat the pattern, leaving behind seemingly bewildered guards.

A number of other fish frequently join these feeding aggregations. Most commonly, these include other herbivores like the midnight parrotfish. But it is not unusual for a few carnivores to join in, possibly to take advantage of small reef animals dislodged or exposed by the feeding activities of the plant-eaters. Group feeding among the surgeonfishes may also function to deter predators.

Figure 4-3. A large feeding aggregation of blue tang. (Photo: W. Alevizon.)

Chubs. The final group of large roving plant-eaters common on Caribbean reefs are the swift, schooling chubs. True nomads, these regularly cross expanses of sand and seagrass to visit different reefs. It is not uncommon to find a particular reef area chub-less for days, and then suddenly find oneself surrounded by a large school. Although considered herbivores, these fish also sometimes eat considerable amounts of animal material. It is not known if animals are swallowed incidentally, or actively hunted.

Because chubs range so widely they are difficult to study, and relatively little is known about their habits. On one occasion, I witnessed what appeared to be an enormous spawning aggregation over a reef face in the Bahamas in water depths of about 30–50 feet. The mass of fish extended from the surface to the reef below, and farther than the eye could see. I snorkeled for some distance in an attempt to find the limits, but the sea of chubs seemed to go on well beyond my desire to swim to its end. Fish numbered in the thousands, with individuals hovering just a foot to several feet away from one another. Spawning was not observed, but the entire scene was highly reminiscent of grouper spawning aggregations that occur in these same waters. The possibility of accidentally stumbling across seldom observed events such as this is one of the most alluring facets of reef exploration.

Sedentary Herbivores—Damselfishes. These fishes [Figure 4-4] represent an alternative mode of plant eating—they are the "farmers" of the reef. In terms of numbers of individuals, there is no doubt that they are the ruling herbivores of Caribbean reef areas. Damselfishes are small, usually no more than three or four inches in length. Most species have highly similar body shapes, and many bear similar hues as adults. As is often the case with reef fishes, juveniles tend to have quite different coloration than adults. Damselfishes are common in almost all reef and reef-type environments, including rocky shores and jetties.

Some members of this family hunt in the open waters above the reef for tiny zooplankton; these will be discussed later. Here we will consider the small territorial species that remain close to the reef, tending and nibbling at their jealously guarded little vegetable gardens. Some species actually kill the coral polyps in a small area to allow for the settlement and growth of their algal food source. Because they are so aggressive in defending their areas, damselfishes tend to be spaced rather evenly over the reef. This is distinctly different from the "patchy" distribution pattern characteristic of more socially inclined or schooling species (e.g., grunts, snappers) that tend to occur in large groups in just a few places.

Figure 4-4. The juvenile yellowtail damselfish. (Photo: Graham Teague.)

Damselfishes spend a good deal of time and energy dealing with roving herbivores that might otherwise steal their food. Aggressive behavior is frequently directed mainly at other plant eaters, while carnivores are allowed to pass freely in and out of the territories. However, damselfishes will quite aggressively attempt to chase divers, boldly nipping at hair or even skin. Perhaps this is because they do not know what the eating habits of people are, and so are taking no chances.

These small warriors are not in the least deterred by the size of the intruder; parrotfish that could conceivably swallow a damsel whole are viciously attacked, and with great success. Why do such large fish react at all to these tiny terrors? The answer is unknown, but it certainly seems curious because it is unlikely that a small damselfish has the capacity to inflict real damage on such foes.

Damselfishes are an unusual exception to the "shotgun" approach to reproduction generally employed by reef fishes. Rather than spewing huge numbers of eggs into the plankton, they produce fewer, larger eggs that adhere in clusters to the reef surface. The eggs are vigorously guarded from would-be predators, and the parents use fin movements to assure that the developing young are continually bathed by fresh oxygen-rich water. Newly hatched damselfishes are therefore likely to grow up in the same neighborhood inhabited by the parents. They also stand a much better chance of surviving to adulthood than do their planktonic counterparts.

Others. A few other common and widespread groups of Caribbean reef fishes contain some members that at least on occasion consume considerable quantities of plant material. These include most notably the blennies and angelfishes. A better understanding of the nutritional role of plant material in these species awaits further study.

FISH THAT EAT PLANKTON

Considering the rich source of food the plankton often represents on the reef, it is not surprising that some reef fishes have evolved to become exclusive plankton feeders, and that this way of life has shaped both their bodies and their behaviors to the extent that they are now quite different from close relatives that feed in other ways.

To gain access to plankton before it is decimated by the feeding activities of corals and other reef creatures, these fishes must necessarily distance themselves somewhat from the immediate shelter of the reef [Figure 4-5]. Many achieve a measure of safety from even larger predators by seeking safety in numbers, a traditional defense of open-water fishes. Plankton feeders also rely on speed, and many have acquired sleeker lines than those

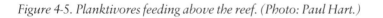

Figure 4-5. Planktivores feeding above the reef. (Photo: Paul Hart.)

possessed by their bottom feeding relatives. Color patterns have been modified as well. Plankton feeders are generally clad in monochromatic blue or silver, color schemes that reduce their chances of detection in the open sea. Other adaptations include sharp eyesight, keen reactions, and small, protrusible jaws suited to capture and handle a variety of tiny prey.

Unlike most of the other feeding types discussed, reef-dwelling planktivores are not represented by entire families that have specialized in a particular way of life. Instead, the plankton-feeding fraternity of Caribbean reefs consists of a hodgepodge of distantly related groups.

Several damselfishes are beautifully adapted for plankton feeding. These are the blue and brown chromis, two small, highly similar species with streamlined bodies and simple color schemes [Figure 4-6a]. *Chromis* are common on both deep and shallow reefs throughout the Caribbean. They are nearly always associated with others of their kind when feeding, and like many planktivores, will descend quickly into the safety of the reef if they feel threatened. Another damselfish often seen feeding above shallow reefs is the *sergeant major,* a larger relative that feeds on benthic algae as well as on plankton. This species has retained the traditional damselfish shape and bears a more complex color pattern.

Figure 4-6. The blue chromis (a) has come to look much like the creole wrasse (b), and shares much the same life style. (Photo (a): Doug Perrine; Photo (b): Graham Teague.)

a

The *creole wrasse* [Figure 4-6b] is from a very different heritage than the blue chromis, but the demands of their similar plankton-feeding lifestyles have resulted in two species alike enough in size, shape, and color that they are easily and frequently confused. The creole wrasse eventually attains larger size than the blue chromis, but similar-sized individuals of the two species often form mixed aggregations when feeding.

Less frequently, a third species clad in much the same hues joins in as well. This is the *boga,* a slender cigar-shaped fish. The boga is much more sporadic in occurrence than these other two, and if present is only seen near the outer reef margins. It probably spends much or most of its time farther offshore, and thus might be more properly considered a visitor to reef areas rather than a resident.

Another notable plankton feeder is the *yellowtail snapper,* a sleek streamlined fish much more jack-like than snapper-like in outward appearance [Figure 4-7]. As it grows, this fish feeds ever more heavily on other fishes and less on plankton. It is curious, and will readily follow divers about.

The *scrawled filefish* on the other hand is anything but sleek and swift. This unlikely planktivore provides amusing fish-watching opportunities as it picks at tiny drifting prey. The bold, brightly speckled color pattern and odd positioning of the body give it somewhat of a clownish look. It gener-

b

Figure 4-7. The yellowtail snapper—a swift open water hunter. (Photo: Paul Hart.)

ally remains very close to the surface where its colors blend with the bright shifting patterns created by sunlight dancing off the waves.

A not-too-distant relative, the *black durgeon,* is a wary and far less common member of the plankton feeding fraternity. A seeming "gourmet" among reef planktivores, it is most particular in its choice of dining places, and is generally found in small groups at just a few select spots on the upper reef face. It remains faithful to these chosen places, and may be found there regularly.

Some planktivores do not seek out the "hot spots" of plankton influx on their reefs, but instead simply take advantage of "leftovers" reaching their homes. An example of this type of plankton feeder is the *fairy basslet,* a strikingly beautiful little fish that remains at all times very close to the small patch of reef it calls home. These always keep their bellies directly toward the reef surface, and seem quite comfortable living upside down below coral ledges.

Also an advocate of the waiting game is the little *yellowhead jawfish,* which makes its own home by digging a small burrow in the sand near the base of lagoonal patch reefs [Figure 4-8]. It hovers just above the sand to feed,

Figure 4-8. A yellowhead jawfish hovers above its home. (Photo: Graham Teague.) ▶

Figure 4-9. A night planktivore—the cardinalfish. (Photo: Doug Perrine.)

and if danger is sensed the fish backs quickly tail-first into its refuge, where it remains until the coast is clear. Several of the territorial damselfishes generally described as herbivores also sometimes feed on passing plankton while remaining in their usual close proximity to the reef.

The fishes discussed here take shelter after the sun goes down, for the kinds of eyes that function to provide sharp vision in brightly lit waters are poorly suited to seeing at night. As they retire for the evening, the daytime planktivores leave behind a rich untapped food source. Such opportunities are rarely wasted on the reef, and after dark a "night shift" of plankton-feeding fishes becomes active. This group most notably includes cardinalfish, some squirrelfish, and the sweepers. These night feeders remain concealed in the reef by day, often within the same cavities that now hide the daylight planktivores [Figure 4-9].

5

HUNTERS OF
INVERTEBRATE PREY

PROWLERS OF THE SEAFLOOR

We will now take a closer look at some of the carnivorous fishes common to Caribbean reefs. In this chapter, we consider those that feed mainly on invertebrate animals of the seafloor. Animals that live on (or in) the bottom of the sea are termed *benthic,* and those that feed on them are called benthic carnivores, or *benthivores* for short. Although fish and invertebrate prey may be benthic in habit, the term "benthivore" generally refers only to predators that feed on invertebrate prey.

Benthivores have an impressive array of prey to choose from in Caribbean reef environments. On the surface, one might be tempted to believe that such food resources are so varied and plentiful that they could be neatly divided up among the different kinds of fishes, so that each had its own special food and no need to use those of others. But that's just not the way it is. Apparently, the best way to make a living as a reef benthivore is to pick a place and time to hunt, and then eat everything possible. Of course, different kinds of benthivores have different abilities, behaviors and feeding structures, and the kinds of prey they commonly eat reflects this to some extent. Still, many are quite generalized in their food habits.

Reef habitats require somewhat different hunting strategies and equipment than do off-reef habitats, just as feeding during the day requires different adaptations than those needed for hunting at night. With few exceptions then, benthivores primarily feed in just one of several possible ways. Let's consider in turn each of these ways of "benthivoring."

DAY BENTHIVORES OF REEF HABITATS

Whether on the reef or in sand, the rule of survival for most small invertebrates is to stay well-hidden during the daylight hours. Particularly on the reef, there are simply too many pairs of sharp eyes attached to hungry mouths waiting to catch sight of a vulnerable little snack. An invertebrate going for a mid-morning swim in this situation is about as safe as a person strolling down the Santa Monica freeway at rush hour. Wisely, prey do not often make things that easy for their predators.

Some benthic invertebrates do not have the option of hiding. Large colonial animals, such as gorgonians and sponges, must rely on other defenses. Smaller forms that are accessible during the day are usually very well camouflaged, requiring sharp eyes for detection. Once found, they may be tightly attached to the reef. Even when removed, they are no easy meal. Most have defenses—thick shells, sharp spines, or noxious chemicals to turn away would-be diners. Many small animals remain deep within nooks and crannies of the reef, places unavailable to all but the tiniest benthivores.

To feed successfully on the reef by day then, benthivores need some special abilities. Highly precise swimming movements are required to reach and pull prey from minimally accessible hiding places. Such prey often must be forcibly dislodged by being grasped and pulled. Good close vision is required not only to locate prey, but also to unerringly guide the fine maneuvering needed for capture. Special mouths are necessary, capable of plucking the victim from its refuge and then crushing the shell or dealing with other defenses. Finally, day benthivores that are out and about for long periods, with attention riveted on the business of finding and capturing food, must have means of defending themselves from even larger hunters.

These requirements may well have led to the evolution of an entire order of reef fishes particularly well-adapted to hunt the reef by daylight. These are the *puffers* and their relatives the *filefish, triggerfish, trunkfish,* and *porcupinefish* [Figure 5-1]. They are almost exclusively occupants of reef habitats. Most species

Figure 5-1. Daytime hunters of the reef include the triggerfish (a), porcupinefish (b), and trunkfish (c). (Photos: Graham Teague.) ▶

feed heavily on benthic invertebrates—particularly the shelled kind—and so possess stout teeth or beaklike mouths. They also have unusually strong jaw muscles and inner (pharyngeal) teeth to deal with the armor of such prey.

These fishes have acquired effective methods of deterring predation. Puffers take in water when threatened and make themselves too large to swallow. Filefish and triggerfish have extremely stout spines on their backs— in triggerfishes these lock into place, enabling them to wedge themselves irretrievably into the reef. Porcupinefish turn their bodies into large pincushions by combining an array of sharp stout spines with the ability to distend their bodies by swallowing water. Puffers perform the same trick, but lacking the spines, they have developed powerful toxins as an additional deterrent. Trunkfish have developed a coat of heavy external armor composed of fused bony plates as their primary defense.

Reliance on defenses other than speed has allowed the group to take on odd body shapes and develop an unusual swimming style, one that emphasizes the highly coordinated use of all the fins to achieve extremely precise movement. All in all then, this unusual group of reef fishes is beautifully adapted to the requirements of feeding on benthic invertebrates by day, and they are the true masters of this strategy. Still, it seems that the life of a large diurnal benthivore must be a tough one—these fishes occur in rather low numbers in comparison with most of the groups that feed in other ways.

There is also a group of small and rather sedentary fishes that spends the daylight hours hunting tiny prey among the algae and corals. Many of these are cryptic in both habit and appearance as well, and thus comparatively little is known about their feeding behavior. The *seahorse* [Figure 5-2] admirably exemplifies this group, which also includes the abundant little blennies and gobies. It is known that many *blennies* [Figure 5-3] supplement their diets with algae, while many *gobies* [Figure 5-4] are cleaners, feeding upon the parasites of other fishes.

Two other groups that might also well be included here are the *hamlets* and *wrasses*. The hamlets [Figure 5-5] are small relatives of the groupers that seldom stray from the proximity of the reef. They are generalized carnivores that eat small invertebrates, and occasionally small fishes as well. There remains a long-standing debate regarding the different color patterns seen within the group. Do they represent the badges of different species, or simply a variable scheme worn by members of a single species? There appear to be differences in the behaviors and distributions among differently hued hamlets, but these are difficult to define or measure. Perhaps the most objective evidence that may be applied here is that the varieties appear to interbreed successfully. Based on this, current opinion favors the view that the hamlets in all their guises represent but a single species.

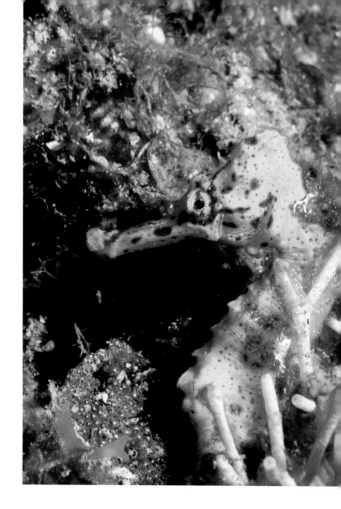

Figure 5-2. The seahorse is well camouflaged. (Photo: Graham Teague.)

Figure 5-3. A blenny contemplates the world from safety. (Photo: Holly Hart.)

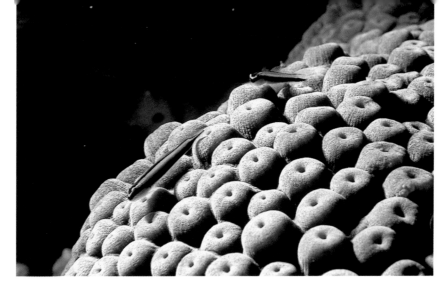

Figure 5-4. Gobies are often cleaners of other fishes. (Photo: Graham Teague.)

Figure 5-5. Hamlets are smaller versions of their close relatives the groupers. (Photo: Graham Teague.)

Wrasses are found in just about all reef and off-reef habitats. Most are small cigar-shaped fishes [Figure 5-6], and all are strict carnivores. They share with their close allies the parrotfishes the same unusual life history pattern, characterized by radical changes in appearance upon undergoing a mid-life sex-reversal. True daytime fishes, most wrasses sleep the night away beneath

Figure 5-6. Wrasses are carnivorous cousins of the parrotfishes. (Photo: Holly Hart.)

the sand at the base of the reef. Some species feed on the reef proper, while others hunt in nearby off-reef habitats.

Rather than searching for and consuming entire prey, there is another quite different way to feed on the reef as a benthivore. It is possible to go around nipping off the exposed parts of animals that are too large or too well protected to fall prey in their entirety. An advantage of this strategy is that the food resources are highly visible and generally plentiful. Thus, almost no time need be spent searching for prey.

The closely related *butterflyfishes* and *angelfishes* [Figure 5-7] have become specialized for just that tactic. Although both employ the same basic strategy, each concentrates on somewhat different prey. Butterflyfish nip coral polyp tentacles and the feeding tentacles of worms and such, while angelfish browse heavily on sponges, and often algae as well. Both have mouths designed for this sort of feeding. The butterflyfish is particularly adept, with fine brush-like teeth set in jaws that often resemble surgical forceps. In both groups, resident "couples" remain together for extended periods, perhaps for life.

These are brightly colored fishes. Butterflyfish often bear an *ocellus,* or eye-spot, prominently displayed on the dorsal part of the body. In general,

a

b

Figure 5-7. Butterflyfish (a) and angelfish (b) browse the reef by daylight. (Photos: Graham Teague.)

such adornments are called *deflective marks,* and are believed to reduce the owner's chances of prematurely ending its days as the meal of another. Deflective marks may function in several ways to that end. When combined with coloration that conceals the real eye, they may confuse would-be predators. Successful attack requires anticipation of the prey's evasive reaction. If the tail of the prey is mistaken for the head, a predator will "lead" its target in the wrong direction.

Deflective marks are also used to direct attacks away from vital areas of the body to less vulnerable parts. Divers frequently observe reef fish with bite-shaped pieces missing, particularly from the back. Often, the wound has healed over nicely and the fish seems to be doing just fine. These are the lucky survivors of attacks by would-be predators; such strikes would be fatal in the head region. The eye-spot of the butterflyfish presumably functions to at least give it a chance of escaping even after being "hit." Several other reef fishes, particularly damselfishes, possess eye-spots only as juveniles, a time when they are most vulnerable to visual predators.

DAY BENTHIVORES OF OFF-REEF HABITATS

Life in the open, away from the shelter of the reef, requires some specialized abilities. There are some benthivores particularly adapted for life in off-reef habitats—the mojarras, some wrasses, flatfish, and the rays [Figure 5-8]

Figure 5-8. The stingray presents a low profile, and is well-armed. (Photo: Graham Teague.)

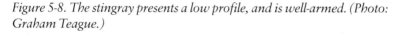

are such fish. But it is no surprise that few true reef-dwellers venture this way by daylight. Those that do must first and foremost protect themselves from larger predators that roam these areas [Figure 5-9]. Another problem is that few invertebrate prey dare expose themselves in sand or seagrass areas by day. Those that do have shells that are not easily circumvented, unless you happen to be a bulldozer or a brontosaurus. These are things like helmets, whelks, and, of course, the conchs. The vast majority of edible benthic invertebrates that inhabit such places are now buried beneath the sand. In general then, we might well say that off-reef areas are a relatively poor place for reef-dwelling benthivores to feed during the day—food is difficult to find, and the feeder is exposed to the threat of higher predators. Even so, there are a few reef fishes that feed in this way.

The *goatfishes* and some of the *drums* are specialized for feeding in sand [Figure 5-10]. They achieve safety by remaining relatively close to home. It is common to see goatfish foraging near the base of the reef, probing the sand with food-finding appendages called *barbels*. Located on the chin, these detect prey by taste as well as touch.

The *trunkfish* is the rare reef fish unafraid to venture far into off-reef areas in broad daylight, and with good reason. There are few predators capable

Figure 5-9. A lemon shark on the prowl in a shallow seagrass bed. (Photo: Doug Perrine.)

Figure 5-10. The goatfish feeds in the sand but remains close to the reef. (Photo: Louisa Preston.)

of dealing with its armor. The trunkfish locates prey in the sand by searching for tell-tale signs of life, and then excavating the suspect area with jets of water expelled through the mouth.

The *hogfish* [Figure 5-11], largest of the Caribbean wrasses, achieves safety through sheer size—it is just too large for most predators to handle. This fish has jaws and teeth with crushing abilities suited to handling armored prey. But these are exceptions. Most reef dwellers wisely wait for darkness before leaving the comparative safety of the reef to feed elsewhere.

NIGHT BENTHIVORES OF OFF-REEF HABITATS

Within the sediments of sand flats and seagrass beds there is ample room to hide countless hordes of tiny creatures. Seagrass beds provide a rich food source for invertebrates and house the most, but surprising numbers may also inhabit sand or mud bottoms that support little visible plant life. These creatures hide from the eyes of hungry fish during the day, but

Figure 5-11. The hogfish is large enough to feed off the reef in comparative safety. (Photo: J. Halas.)

emerge after dark to feed on plankton, occasional plant life, and one an-other. This creates a real banquet for a group of reef fishes designed to use these rich food resources.

Vision is of minimal utility at night, perhaps permitting the detection of the occasional flash of light produced by living creatures, or the dim recog-nition of prey when the moon is bright. So night benthivores must instead rely heavily on other senses—touch, taste, smell, and the lateral line. These enable the hunter to locate prey in the dark, but not with the same precision possible using vision. Night benthivores then must judge the approximate position of the prey, and then launch an attack that will be effective even if a bit off the mark. They do this by suddenly expanding the large mouth cav-ity, creating a sudden and powerful vacuum that draws water and anything suspended in it right into the mouth. The mouth is then quickly closed, and the water expelled through the gill openings—but only after it has passed through a strainer that retains the prey. It is no coincidence that most noc-turnal benthivores of these areas possess large inhaling-type mouths rather than the smaller picking/grasping-type mouths characteristic of daytime reef benthivores [Figure 5-12].

a

b

Figure 5-12. The mouths of night benthivores [a] differ notably from those of day benthivores [b]. [Photos: Holly Hart.]

The main groups feeding in this way are the *grunts, snappers, squirrelfish,* and *bigeyes.* The grunts and some of the snappers have similar behavioral patterns, so we shall consider these close relatives together. These fish shelter on the reef in loose aggregations throughout the day [Figure 5-13]. Around sunset, they form traveling schools and stream away to the foraging areas. Some are known to swim as far as half a mile or so, following "trails" along the bottom. Upon arrival at the feeding site, they disperse to feed in solitude throughout the night. Well before first light, the schools reassemble and return to the home reef along the same trails.

Squirrelfish, bigeyes, and the small cardinalfish are more ostensibly adapted for the night life [Figure 5-14]. Their large black eyes have supe-

Figure 5-13. Night benthivores sheltering on the reef. [Photo: Paul Hart.]

a   Figure 5-14. The bigeye [a] and squirrelfish [b] display the large black eyes and red colors of true night fishes. [Photos: Graham Teague.]

rior light-gathering abilities, and their reddish colors appear black under low-light conditions. These, particularly the cardinalfish, are secretive during the daylight hours, so there is little indication of the incredible number of individuals tucked away in the reef at that time. Many cardinalfish and some squirrelfish feed as planktivores above and around the reef, while the others are benthivores, some in off-reef areas. These generally remain close to the reef, however, and do not undergo the extensive migrations of the grunts and snappers.

b

Figure 5-14. Continued.

NIGHT BENTHIVORES OF THE REEF

Much of the prey used by benthivores on the reef during the day is still there at night. But the night is a poor time for visually-oriented feeders. Consequently, Caribbean reefs are for the most part devoid of benthivores between the hours of dusk and dawn. The few that comb the reef after dark feed much in the same manner as night benthivores of off-reef habitats—inhaling rather than picking prey from the substrate.

6

FISH THAT EAT
OTHER FISH

THE TOP PREDATORS

The most notorious of all reef fishes are the *piscivores*—those that prey on their comrades. Despite their unsavory reputation, these creatures are in truth a far cry from their popularized image of bloodthirsty insatiable monsters bent upon the destruction of anything that moves beneath the sea—including swimmers and divers. The larger predators tend to be curious, but readily recognize that people are not on their menus. Some are certainly quite capable of inflicting serious damage on humans, but such incidents are extremely rare, particularly when one considers the vast number of encounters in which this type of behavior could be exhibited.

This is not surprising from an ecological standpoint because violent behavior in these creatures is for use against particular targets in specific situations—the taking of prey, or the protection of themselves or their territories. They turn on people only when people are perceived as a threat or mistaken for prey. Contrary to popular myth, they do not bite people just for fun or because it's in their nature.

There are three basic strategies employed by reef predators hunting other fishes. We shall examine these one at a time, but first we will consider some general aspects of predator-prey interactions among reef fishes.

THE USE OF SHELTER

Were it not for the shelter provided by the reef itself, marauding predators would have an easy time of it, literally feeding at will on slower smaller species that call the reef home. The agility that characterizes reef fishes serves them well only when afforded the protection of solid objects about which to maneuver. Shelter in this sense is not used to conceal the prey, but rather to confound the mechanism of high-speed attacks. Predators that approach prey from a distance accelerate rapidly during the actual attack, which is made at very high speed. Such predators are also agile, and quite capable of making adjustments during the final stages of the attack to compensate for escape reactions of their prey. Thus, alertness and quickness are not in themselves necessarily successful defenses. But if movement of the victim places something solid in the line of attack, either in front of or close behind, the swiftly approaching predator must break off the attack or risk breaking off its face!

For these reasons, most reef fish tend to remain close enough to the reef to allow them to use it effectively in this manner, never straying so far to allow speedy predators a sufficiently unobstructed "line of fire" [Figure 6-1]. In general, larger size permits greater swimming speed in fishes. This means that as a rule small fish must remain closer to the reef than larger fish, because this allows them to reach safety in time.

Figure 6-1. Reef fish achieve protection by remaining close to the reef. [Photo: Paul Hart.]

THE TWILIGHT ADVANTAGE

An interesting discovery regarding some reef piscivores involves their vision. It had been noted for some time that many seemed to hunt much more actively around the hours of sunrise and sunset. Close examination of the eyes of reef fishes has confirmed part of the reason why this is a successful strategy.

For most reef fishes, the gathering of sufficient food in the forms of plants or small, well-hidden invertebrates requires that much time be invested in these activities. There are only two sufficiently lengthy periods available to such foragers—day and night. As we have seen, there are advantages and disadvantages to feeding at either time, and not surprisingly, there are two corresponding "sets" of reef fishes, one adapted to be active by day, and the other by night. Daytime fishes have eyes that function best under well-lit conditions, while night fishes have eyes especially suited to vision under very low levels of light.

Predators have used this simple fact to their hunting advantage, developing eyes that work better than those of their fish prey during the two brief periods when it is neither bright nor dark—the hours of sunrise and sunset. Dawn and dusk are most dangerous times for reef fishes, and this has led to a regular cycle of events on the reef that accompanies the transitions between day and night. We will use the sunset period to illustrate this phenomenon.

About an hour before the sun fades below the horizon, daylight fishes begin to gather close to the reef, seeking its shelter ever more closely. At this time, sand and seagrass areas become noticeably empty of fish life. Just prior to sunset, daytime fishes begin to actually settle into their nighttime refuges.

This leads to a so-called "quiet period" lasting from about 10–15 minutes before sunset to about 30 minutes after. This is a time when it is just too dangerous to risk exposure. Predators have taken up hunting positions close to the seafloor, where they wait in the deepening twilight to spot a careless victim silhouetted against the surface of the sea. The quiet period ends as the night fishes begin to emerge from hiding, and soon after the feeding migrations into nearby seagrass habitats begin.

THE HUNTERS OF FISH

Let us now consider the main strategies employed by reef fishes that feed on others. Three types of hunters may be distinguished. *Pursuing predators* begin their attacks from a moving start, and from relatively long range—perhaps at the point where visual contact is first possible. *Stalking preda-*

tors initiate their attack from a hovering or drifting position, making no sudden or direct threat until stealth and camouflage have allowed them to achieve close striking range—often no more than a few body lengths. *Ambush predators* engage in little or no preliminary maneuvering. These literally make themselves part of the reef or surrounding seafloor, using near-perfect disguise to take prey by sudden surprise. Attack is made in the form of a quick strike with no warning, and initiated from a standing start at extremely close range—often less than a single body length.

Pursuing Predators

Some hunters habitually attack other fish from a considerable distance, relying on sheer speed to run down the victim in open waters above the reef. This is the least subtle but perhaps most dramatic method of hunting other fishes. Pursuing predators in Caribbean waters include most notably certain of the *sharks, jacks, mackerels,* and the *yellowtail snapper.* These are all swift, sleek fishes that swim more or less continuously over a large home range and are capable of great bursts of speed.

Pursuing predators vary to some extent in the degree to which they have compromised the "perfect" speed design with other needs. Nonetheless, the fact that they are all built for swift, sustained movement has resulted in some strikingly similar characteristics among distant relatives [Figure 6-2]. All tend toward an efficient torpedo-shaped body. External irregularities such as scales, fins, gill coverings, etc. that would cause drag are reduced to an absolute minimum and designed to follow the body contours. For example, the scales of jacks and mackerels are tiny, and embedded in the skin so as to produce a uniform smooth exterior.

The tail regions of such fishes are uncannily similar, and for good reasons. The caudal fin is sickle-shaped, like the swept-back wings of a jet fighter. This is the best shape to provide thrust (or lift in the case of the jet), and at the same time minimize drag at high speed. The fin itself is stiffer than in most other fishes. These elements of design act in concert to allow the tail to be vibrated rapidly and efficiently, creating strong propulsion with little turbulence. Additionally, the *caudal peduncle* (region just forward of the caudal fin) is very narrow, and frequently bears a laterally-projecting keel on each side to aid in turning at high speeds.

The most common pursuing predators on Caribbean reefs are several members of the jack family, and the yellowtail snapper. Jacks come in range of sizes. Small bar jacks are the most often encountered, but several larger species are not uncommon visitors to Caribbean reefs [Figure 6-3].

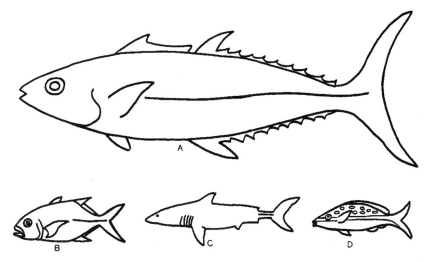

Figure 6-2. *The body plan of the pursuing predator is exemplified by the mackerel (a). The same basic design elements are seen in the jacks (b), sharks (c), and yellowtail snapper (d). (Illustrations: Ruth Rasche.)*

Figure 6-3. *Horse-eye jacks sweep across the reef in search of fish prey. (Photo: Doug Perrine.)*

These typically move through quickly in small hunting "packs," scanning the water column for easy meals. As these "heavy hitters" move about the reef, there is a noticeable change in activity patterns among smaller reef fishes, a sudden wariness and sense of danger that is perceptible even to divers. Occasionally, representatives of the ultra-sleek mackerels may be seen as well. These relatives of the tunas are the ultimate speed machines of the fish world. They tend to frequent the deep reef face, patrolling its edge for stray fish and squid.

The yellowtail snapper is particularly common, feeding on plankton when small and on fishes when larger. It is possible that small planktivorous fishes are made more vulnerable to this particular predator through constant exposure to its presence. The yellowtail snapper is a curious fish, and will frequently follow divers.

Sharks are not everyday sights on most Caribbean reefs [Figure 6-4]. Most are shy and will quickly leave an area upon noting the presence of divers. The most common by far is the nurse shark, a night prowler that spends most of the day resting under ledges.

Figure 6-4. A cruising shark—a sight all too rare on Caribbean reefs. (Photo: Graham Teague.)

Stalking Predators

A different group of predators employs quite another strategy, using stealth and camouflage to allow the final attack to be initiated at relatively close range. This is the stalking approach to fish hunting, and Caribbean reefs are home to some unrivaled masters of the technique. As with pursuing predators, the requirements of this strategy have led to notable physical and behavioral similarities among those who employ it. Typically, stalking predators have elongate bodies that present minimal profiles when positioned to strike [Figure 6-5]. Additionally, because the attack takes the form of a short swift movement, the posterior fins of these fishes are configured and function much like the symmetrical vanes of an arrow. The caudal fin has a relatively large surface area, providing rapid acceleration with just a few powerful strokes.

The *trumpetfish* is particularly worth watching, for unlike many of the other stalkers, it actively hunts throughout the day. Additionally, it seems little affected by the presence of fish-watchers, so long as proper distance is maintained. There are at least three color variants, with the most common by far being a mottled, rusty-hued type. Bright yellow fish are not infrequent, while a deep blue variety is the most rare. These appear to be color varieties in much the same manner seen in the hamlets. Limited research indicates

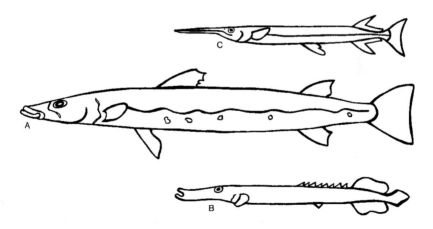

Figure 6-5. The body plan of stalking predators is illustrated by the barracuda (a). The trumpetfish (b) and houndfish (c) have similar forms. (Illustrations: Ruth Rasche.)

that individuals are not capable of switching from one color to another, at least not in a matter of minutes or hours.

This fish is unmatched in its clever use of cover. It aligns its slender body with gorgonians, seeming to disappear. Slowly, it brings the body into alignment with the intended prey, and in that position its body shape alone presents little to betray its presence—it's a bit like looking at a pencil head-on [Figure 6-6]. There is a sudden flick of the tail, a snap of the jaws, and the prey is gone! The closely related *cornetfish* feeds in very much the same manner, but is more a hunter of off-reef habitats.

Figure 6-6. When aligned for attack, the trumpetfish presents a minimum profile. (Photo: Doug Perrine.)

The *barracuda* is probably the Caribbean reef fish most often the cause of alarm among divers and snorkelers [Figure 6-7]. There have been a few recorded instances of aggressive behavior directed at people by these fish. These are often directly attributable to defensive reactions (as when the fish bites a diver who has just speared it, or when divers attempt to dispute the barracuda's claim to a fish speared in its territory). In other biting instances, the barracuda may have confused part of the swimmer or diver with fish prey. This is one good reason why wearing jewelry in the sea is discouraged, particularly that worn around the throat. There are no recorded instances of barracudas using people as food.

The life history of this fish provides a fine illustration of the interrelated roles inshore habitats play in the lives of many reef fishes. Small barracudas inhabit seagrasses and seaweeds along shorelines, in very shallow water. There they feed on a variety of juvenile reef fishes common to such areas. As they grow, they move out to deeper waters of the lagoon, feeding among the hardground and patch reef habitats. The largest individuals are most common on the reef face, and are known to patrol well offshore for passing schools of open-water fishes. At such times they hunt in much the same manner as pursuing predators.

Figure 6-7. A barracuda on patrol. (Photo: Doug Perrine.)

One final stalking predator of note is the *houndfish,* a pale ghostlike creature that hangs just below the surface of the sea above shallow reefs, particularly in the lagoonal patch reef and reef crest habitats. Although sometimes quite large, its habits and coloration make the houndfish nearly invisible, even when only at a distance of a few feet. It remains stationary for a few moments at a time, and then quickly darts a few feet away to take up a new vantage point. When it spots a reef fish a bit too far from cover, it strikes with unerring accuracy and speed.

Ambush Predators

The final strategy that we shall discuss is that of ambush and surprise, in which successful hunting is facilitated by effective disguise coupled with absolute stillness. Ambushers come in a variety of shapes, with sleek lines definitely not an essential part of their anatomies. In one way or another, they all use coloration to achieve near-invisibility, remaining still until the luckless victim is but a quick gulp away. Also to this end, ambush predators have unusually large upward-facing mouths capable of suddenly creating a powerful vacuum.

The most successful by far at this waiting game are the *seabasses*—groupers, hinds, and the like. Some species also sometimes hunt as stalking predators, maneuvering themselves into a superior position for attack. Still, in general the bodies and habits of these fishes are clearly more closely allied with the bushwhacking way of life. Groupers are particularly proficient at blending with the reef background. They are the ultimate inhaling-type predators, lurking motionless in their caves or in the shelter of a coral head as they wait for the next victim to blunder within striking range.

The *scorpionfish* and *toadfish* use much the same strategy, although they have perfected disguises that closely picture their resting places, as opposed to the more generalized disruptive patterns of the groupers. They are therefore more restricted in choice of hunting places, and are faithful residents of the reef proper. Scorpionfish have a strong neurotoxin that may be inflicted by contact with the stout dorsal spines. This is another good reason for divers

Figure 6-8. The scorpionfish (a) and toadfish (b) are perfectly disguised for ambush. (Photo (a): Louisa Preston; photo (b): Holly Hart.) ▶

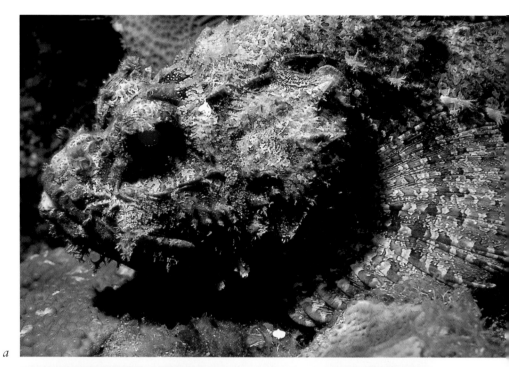

a

b

Figure 6-9. A lizardfish waits in silent ambush. (Photo: Graham Teague.)

to remain well beyond the range of physical contact with the reef at all times, for such dangers are unlikely to be seen until it is too late.

The smaller *lizardfish* is also an ambusher, and often favors rocky outcroppings near the base of the reef, or even the sand itself as its perch from which to hunt [Figure 6-9].

The *flounder* is a creature primarily designed for life in off-reef habitats, but which nonetheless also frequents reef areas and occasionally feeds on reef fish. This amazing fish is able to change color patterns at will to perfectly match its background. Often, it buries itself slightly so that only the eyes and gill cover remain exposed. When a victim strays too close, this "flying carpet" of the sea springs from hiding with amazing swiftness.

7

CORAL REEFS, DIVERS, AND CONSERVATION

We have explored in the preceding chapters just a few of the intricacies involved in the life of a coral community. Modern coral reefs represent the products of millions upon millions of years of evolution and adaptation, processes that have enabled these marvelous cities beneath the sea to sustain themselves through both long and short-term changes in their environmental settings. Despite this remarkable longevity, reefs today are facing unprecedented threats directly linked to the activities and explosive growth of human populations. It seems fitting that we end this book with a discussion of some of the dangers facing the world's coral reefs, and some of the things that may be done by each of us to ensure their continuation.

PROBLEMS

Human activities are not by any means the only perils in the lives of coral reefs—natural disasters may wreak havoc as well.

Natural Threats

If we dive in remote Caribbean locations, far from human population centers and sources of pollution, we may still view Caribbean reefs much as they have existed for millions of years. While these reefs are pristine, they are quite obviously not free from damage. Coral colonies are regularly injured or killed by a variety of "natural" phenomena. The most dramatic of these are of course the devastating effects of the large tropical storms and hurricanes that regularly sweep through this part of the world. The powerful waves generated by such storms topple large colonies hundreds of years old, and tumble them about like so many toys. These coral juggernauts in turn crush and scrape other colonies, leaving a trail of destruction in their wakes. Sediments raised and swept violently across reef areas scour and scrape the bases of coral

Figure 7-1. The base of a coral colony damaged by sand scouring. (Photo: Graham Teague.)

colonies [Figure 7-1] and are deposited among the living polyps, smothering them. Even after the storm has subsided the danger yet remains, for injured areas may now be highly vulnerable to infection by bacteria or colonization by rapidly growing algae, processes that in time may kill the entire colony. It is seldom appreciated that a direct "hit" by a hurricane will cause coral damage of far greater extent than the grounding of a large ship.

Natural processes that occur over decades or centuries may lead to similar results. Current patterns may shift, causing changes in the shapes of shorelines, or the building and erosion of sand bars. If areas once bathed by sparkling blue seas in time become subjected to waters clouded with sediments, entire reefs may be destroyed. Naturally occurring long-term changes in temperatures or rainfall patterns may also create conditions that stress corals, sometimes causing a phenomenon known as "bleaching" in which colonies lose their characteristic hues and turn a chalky white [Figure 7-2]. On a grander scale, long-term changes in sea level have periodically led to the destruction and creation of entire regions of reef development.

Figure 7-2. Coral bleaching may result from high water temperatures. (Photo: John Halas.)

Thus, even without our interference, coral reefs are far from immune to catastrophic damage. However, a point worth considering in this context is that our perception of "damage" may be sometimes misleading. Many ecosystems have calamities to deal with on a periodic basis—the forest has its fires and the desert its flash floods. We do not fully understand the significance of such events in terms of ecosystem function, but we have begun to appreciate the fact that these ecosystems have developed with regular exposure to such events, and, at least in some cases, such natural "disasters" may in subtle ways actually confer certain benefits to ecosystems in addition to the superficially obvious destruction they often wreak.

Human Threats

The obvious differences between "natural" and human damage to reefs is that the latter case is under our direct control, and often consists of stresses to which coral reefs have never been exposed. For this reason, it is essential for anyone concerned with the health of coral reefs to be aware of the nature of *anthropogenic* (people-induced) threats to coral reefs, as well as courses of action available to those who would protect them.

Pollutants. Some of the most serious threats to reefs posed by humanity tend to be activities or processes never before encountered through the long evolutionary history of coral reefs—for these, there are no natural defenses. For example, massive discharges of chemical pollutants into coastal waters areas may have lethal and widespread effects on reef areas. A compounding factor in many cases is that unlike the effects of ship groundings and hurricanes, the results of many forms of pollution are not immediately obvious; the damage may not become apparent for years, and by then it may be beyond repair.

A form of pollution particularly harmful to reefs is the discharge of nutrient-rich waste waters into coastal marine environments. Under normal circumstances, a limited nutrient supply coupled with the feeding of herbivores acts to limit algal growth. But waters laden with nitrates from sewage or fertilizers may lead to explosive plant growth, well beyond the capacity of the hungriest of herbivores to counteract. Thick algal mats may then literally smother the reef [Figure 7-3]. Fertilizers and pesticides from farmlands far inland may percolate for many miles through porous soils to eventually emerge in reef areas, with the same effects.

Figure 7-3. Uncontrolled algal growth resulting from nutrient overload. (Photo: John Halas.)

Thermal Pollution. Excess heating of seawater is also a serious concern. Until recently, this was believed a threat only on a local scale, where electric or industrial plants discharged heated effluents into the sea. But now there is evidence suggesting that a pattern of global warning, possibly induced by human activities, may threaten reefs on a global scale.

Sedimentation. We have seen that adjacent marine habitats are ecologically linked in numerous ways. There are also links between the sea and the land, and ecological processes in marine environments may be substantially affected by things happening hundreds of miles inland. When land is stripped of natural vegetation through clearing and burning, there is little left to hold soils in place. Rains will then carry far greater loads of sediments directly into the sea, or into streams and rivers that eventually lead to the sea.

Similar effects may be produced by activities associated with the urbanization of coastal areas. This often involves dredging boat channels, building marinas, docks, piers and jetties, and sometimes includes the deposition of materials from newly cleared sites directly into the sea. If not properly engineered and controlled, the changes in water quality and movement that typically result from such activities have the capacity to quickly devastate large areas of reef. As we have seen, waters clouded with silt are not conducive to reef growth or survival. Corals vary in their ability to rid themselves of sediments—some are able to deal with limited amounts quite well, but many are not.

Overfishing. Overfishing, particularly through the use of habitat-destructive fishing methods, has decimated reef areas throughout the world. Explosives are sometimes used to stun and kill fish. These may shatter the reef structure, destroying in an instant that which took nature thousands of years to create [Figure 7-4]. The use of chemical poisons, including bleach and soaps, to drive marine life from the reef is common practice

Figure 7-4. A reef devastated by destructive fishing methods. (Photo: Louisa Preston.)

today in many Caribbean island areas, as well as in reef areas throughout much of the Pacific. The removal by any means of excessive numbers of fishes from reef areas may have long-lasting and harmful effects on many aspects of reef ecology—this is an area poorly understood at present.

Boating. Boats may damage reefs directly through physical contact, either by collision, or anchoring on live coral [Figure 7-5]. The end result is the same—corals are crushed, and the door is thrown open to algal and bacterial infection [Figure 7-6]. Boaters may also impact reefs adversely by disposing of wastes overboard—flushing bilges or dumping trash. Although strictly illegal in many waters, such activities are extremely difficult to monitor, and are in fact a common practice aboard many cruising yachts and other vessels.

Figure 7-5. The results of the careless use of anchors (a) and boat collision (b). (Photos: John Halas.)

a

b

Figure 7-5. Continued.

Diving. Divers may directly and indirectly damage reefs in a variety of ways. Physical contact is the most obvious, although it is fair to say that most divers today are warned against this sort of behavior from their first scuba lessons to final pre-dive briefings by divemasters on site. Thus, few modern divers deliberately damage corals in this way, although substantial inadvertent damage occurs from this source due to the insufficient training received by most divers in the control of buoyancy. Unfortunately, underwater photographers seem to be the worst offenders in this category. Perhaps overly engrossed in their efforts to obtain the "perfect" picture, they seem to be much less aware than the non-photographer of making contact with the reef, and seem to do so much more often [Figure 7-7]. Also unacceptable in protected areas is the common photographer's "trick" of

Figure 7-6. Black-band disease—a bacterial infection that may spread to kill the entire colony. (Photo: John Halas.)

smashing living reef creatures to attract fishes for that great close-up to show the folks back home.

Spearfishing has become a highly controversial issue in terms of diving and conservation. While there is no scientific basis whatsoever to suggest that spearfishing *per se* is inherently harmful to marine environments, there is good reason to believe that spearfishing *around reef areas* is a most undesirable activity from a conservation standpoint. The reasons are fairly obvious. Near "misses" frequently take large chunks out of living coral. Wounded and frightened fish will flee into the shelter of the reef, and often must be forcibly pulled out by hunters braced against, and crushing, living

Figure 7-7. Anything for a good picture. (Photo: Graham Teague.)

polyps. Another serious consequence of spearfishing has to do with the highly selective nature of the activity. Typically, the game consists of the larger piscivores—grouper and snapper. The continued removal of most of the higher predators from reef areas leads to wholesale changes in community composition, with unknown long-term effects.

In fairness, I would point out here that hook-and-line fishing may lead to similar results. Sportfishing also selectively removes a particular segment of the reef fish fauna, and almost invariably increases anchor damage to reef areas. Damage caused by sportfishing may persist long after the fishing is over, because of lost lures and fishing line wrapped about the reef and its creatures. Despite these problems, it has proven far more difficult to regulate sportfishing than spearfishing in reef areas. This is primarily because sportfishing interests have a much larger and more well-organized political advocacy than do sport divers.

Inexperienced divers often inadvertently damage corals by allowing spare regulators and gauge consoles to hang unsecured. This is not only harmful to the reef, it is an amateurish diving practice in any case. Vital and expensive equipment may be easily damaged in this way by making contact with sand or rock substrates. Also, divers often unknowingly cause sedimentation damage to corals by swimming too close to the bottom or dragging their legs—practices that cause the fins to raise clouds of sand and silt that settle on and kill living polyps.

Another ill-advised practice is touching or handling of marine life. Trying to communicate feelings of affection, support, or understanding by touching or feeding fish may be philosophically commendable and satisfying to us, but reef fish do not place much value in "bonding" with other species other than by eating them. Such practices may in fact actually harm the intended "friend." Like corals, reef fishes secrete a protective mucous layer that serves as a barrier to infection and the loss of water to the surrounding sea. Disrupting that barrier by touching the fish may therefore subject the animal to increased risk of infection, as well as increased stress in maintaining water balance. Also, reef fish are surprisingly fast learners as well as opportunistic feeders, and our efforts to befriend them by offering food may lead to lasting behavioral changes that result in increased risk of falling prey themselves, or attempting to use food sources that may be harmful.

As a final note on the impacts of modern sport diving, it would be well to briefly discuss an alarming trend that has become increasingly prevalent during the last few years. Within the competitive world of the resort dive operators of the Caribbean region, the traditional role of the dive supervisor as a nature guide is rapidly giving way to that of a side-show entertainer. It seems most ironic that one of the strongest motivations to engage in scuba diving is that it provides us with an opportunity to leave for a while the artificial worlds we have created. A primary reason for visiting places like coral reefs is to observe wildlife in its natural state. What then is the appeal of making a circus of such places? The sight of frantic clouds of reef fishes vying for a taste of Cheeze-Whiz, or the sight of a barracuda snatching a dead fish from the mouth of a divemaster are cheap carnival tricks, not observations of nature.

The increasingly popular side-show approach to resort diving is directly rooted in two relatively recent developments. First, during the last two decades the sport of reef diving has evolved from the pastime of a comparatively small core of adventurous aficionados to the trendy sport of millions—it is now a highly competitive multi-billion dollar industry. Over the same period, the vast majority of new divers just entering the sport were provided with scuba training and certification standards far less rigorous than those of the past—part of an ill-advised but highly successful effort by commercial interests to rapidly widen a lucrative market. The traditional physical and psychological skills and training necessary to confidence and self-reliance underwater suddenly became secondary to the goal of assuring the industry a maximal number of customers as quickly as possible.

A result of these processes is a real need on the part of today's dive operators to accommodate ever-growing hordes of minimally drown-proofed divers. In an attempt to satisfy this new breed of customer who often lacks the skills and confidence to explore, more and more operators are providing trained fish circuses, often right under the boat. Fish-feeding and other forms of orchestrated underwater displays are increasingly seen by operators as the best way of remaining competitive.

In contrast, the resort scene is witnessing the rapid disappearance of the relatively few remaining operators who take their charges to infrequently visited reefs and, with a bit of advice, turn them loose to explore. Sadly, the most adventurous aspect of reef diving—the opportunity to discover—is disappearing with them.

What does all this have to do with reef conservation? Quite simply, the main problem stems from the fact that masses of unskilled divers concentrated in small areas cause far more damage than do the same number of proficient divers spread out over wider areas. It is a nearly universal practice among dive operators to repeatedly take their boats to a relatively few select spots. These are usually the best dive sites in the area—those with the most spectacular coral formations and the most abundant marine life.

Unfortunately then, the very places that should be given maximal protection are the same places being most rapidly devastated by daily deluges of insufficiently trained scuba divers. The diving industry itself has created this massive problem, and until the problem is acknowledged and addressed the negative impact of sport divers will only continue to increase.

SOLUTIONS

When we consider the number of threats confronting the world's coral reefs, the task of reducing their risk may appear overwhelming. It is not. Collectively, we may do much to improve the likelihood of the continued health and survival of these irreplaceable resources. Whether or not we actually do so is a matter of choice—a personal choice for each of us. Here, we examine some of the most effective avenues available to everyone.

Marine Protected Areas

To whom does the reef belong? In addition to native residents (a group, whether sea life or humans, that has been traditionally accorded the least consideration throughout the history of the Caribbean), reef users will typically include a varied mixture of commercial and sportfishing interests, sport divers, nature-tourism interests, scientists, educators, students, and others. How do we reconcile the needs and desires of these varied factions, and at the same time preserve the health of the ecosystem? This is *not* just a question for developed nations—the days of safety through inaccessibility are pretty much over.

The answer is through proper management. To this end, coral reef parks and protected areas of all description are springing up around the globe. Regardless of their names or locations, all have a common goal—partitioning and regulating these sensitive areas in a manner compatible with *sustainable* multiple uses. To the uninitiated, the concept of a park is simply a delimited area belonging to and open to the public at large. The management of the modern marine protected area is far more complex, however. A general familiarity with the goals and methods of this type of resource management is essential to anyone with a serious interest in reef conservation, for it offers one of the best methods of achieving that objective.

A primary goal of most protected areas is the preservation of *biodiversity,* the rich storehouse of life-forms contained within the area. Another common objective is to provide a refuge for education and scientific research. Such areas often include traditional fishing grounds, and the abilities of those so engaged to sustain their livelihoods must be ensured. And finally, protected areas provide a lasting opportunity for all people to see a part of the planet in much its natural state, an opportunity all too quickly disappearing in non-protected areas.

Management plans, therefore, must consider all these (and often other) requirements, and incorporate them into viable operational schemes. Often, a "core" area of high ecological value is designated and earmarked for highly restricted use. Long overdue, there is at last increasing recognition of the need for the incorporation of zero-impact, zero-consumptive use zones in marine park planning. The concept, although widely accepted by scientists, conservationists, and park managers, still remains under heavy fire from opposing groups. Other areas may be designated as places suited to any number of less restrictive uses, such as commercial fishing. The plan is usually integrated in such a way as to provide ample "buffer zones" that minimize the possibility of adverse effects from the different activities occurring in adjacent areas.

The staff and facilities of marine parks cost money, and levying of user fees is becoming an increasingly common and necessary aspect of this form of natural resource protection. Such fees are appropriate, especially in developing island nations that may lack alternative forms of financial support for conservation efforts. The creation of such areas, along with their necessary fees, should be welcomed rather than bemoaned by the sport diving public, as it assures us of increased opportunities for quality reef diving far into the future. The price of a few beers spent instead on conservation during each dive vacation seems reasonable indeed, considering the alternative.

Regulatory management is an essential tool of modern conservation efforts. Too often, however, the designation of marine protected areas is viewed with alarm and opposition by local residents, who tend to see any form of regulation as an unwanted infringement on their birthrights. It is quite understandable for people to resent intrusions by 'outsiders' who suddenly announce unwelcome restrictions on traditional activities. But it must be understood that the oceans are our common heritage—not the property of any single group of people. How will we be able to sufficiently protect marine resources if the desires or "rights" of a limited segment of humanity is allowed to take precedence over the health of those resources?

Boating and Diving Practices

These are areas where individuals may have the most direct and immediate effect on reef conservation efforts. The damage to reefs caused by boats may be easily avoided in most cases through proper training and regulation of boating activities. Unfortunately, however, there is currently no licensing system for boat operators comparable to that in place for motor vehicles, even though boats may be just as destructive in untrained hands. A working knowledge of local waters (or the willingness to acquire such), as well as the use of extreme caution in known reef areas are the hallmarks of the responsible skipper. These alone would prevent most boat groundings. Anchor damage may be easily prevented either through the use of mooring buoys, or in their absence through the careful selection of suitable patches of sand in which to anchor. These are always available in the lagoon, and with a bit of effort may be usually found on the reef face as well. Recommended practices for conservation-conscious divers include the following:

Taking an Active Role

Do Not—

1. Physically contact the reef or its inhabitants.
2. Spearfish in reef areas.
3. Feed reef life.
4. Remove any part of the reef environment.
5. Raise clouds of sand with your fins.
6. Leave behind any trace of your visit.
7. Continue to patronize or recommend reef-damaging dive operations.

Do—

1. Insist that your dive boat be moored or anchored in areas free of live bottom.
2. Ensure that you and your buddy have all equipment securely and closely attached to your persons.
3. Request that all divers in your party respect these guidelines.
4. Patronize and recommend conservation-conscious dive operations.
5. Report observed damage and violations of law to the proper authorities.

We have seen in this chapter that coral reefs throughout the world are in serious peril from a host of threats. In some cases, remedies seem reasonably straightforward—a matter of training and education. In others, solutions are anything but simple. Conservation often is intimately linked to complex social issues, economic development, and various political considerations. Still, there are means available to anyone who wishes to have a voice in support of reef conservation at the national or international levels. One is through the use of established political channels—registering your support of conservation measures and programs with appropriate government officials and agencies. Strong widespread public support for a first-rate, properly funded national program of marine parks and protected areas is a most effective way of promoting the cause of reef conservation. Another is to actively support non-governmental organizations (NGOs) dedicated to conservation at the international level. Several of these have active coral reef components.

At the local level, individuals may exert a very strong influence over attitudes and policies within the dive industry. If you are an active scuba diver, as I suspect many of the readers of this book are, you may well witness reef-damaging activities first-hand on your next diving vacation [Figure 7-8]. At

Figure 7-8. A thoughtless diver damages a decades-old coral colony. (Photo: Graham Teague.)

a

b

Figure 7-9. Aquatic wastelands (a) or undersea gardens (b)–the choice is ours.
(Photo (a): W. Alevizon; Photo (b): Louisa Preston.)

issue here is what do you do when confronted with such abuses? It is not easy for many of us to personally convey our dissatisfaction with the behavior of others, particularly when these others are strangers. But the alternative is silence—and that is generally interpreted as tacit approval.

You are also in a position to directly influence the nature of sport diving operations throughout the Caribbean. Most dive resorts and dive operators today realize that their financial futures are closely tied to the continued health of reefs in their areas, and act accordingly. But there are still those that operate pretty much as they please, engaging in destructive activities whenever it suits their needs. Regardless of posters and slogans, the simple fact remains that dive resorts and dive boats are businesses—the ultimate goal is to make money.

That is where the individual sport diver has perhaps the greatest leverage. The prospect of lost revenues is an incredibly powerful incentive for businesses to change their ways if that is needed. You do not even need to actually say anything to the offenders here—an army of well-informed sport divers that supports and patronizes responsible dive operations and shuns the others is a most effective way of ensuring good conservation practices throughout the industry. In this context it should be recognized that it may cost more to run an environmentally sensitive dive resort. Thus, responsible dive operations may need to charge more than shoddy ones, and supporting reef conservation by patronizing the former may entail minor financial sacrifice on your part.

These are just a few of the ways in which individuals may have a profound positive effect on the future of coral reefs—there are many more. The first step is to make sure that before your next exotic dive trip that *you* have the training, skills, and equipment necessary to be a reef-friendly diver—set an example yourself. We may consider ourselves fortunate to have arrived at a pivotal time in the long saga of coral reefs. We have the opportunity not only to enjoy their beauty, but also to take an active role in assuring that future generations will have the same option. There is still time to preserve and protect these priceless resources if we have the will to do so [Figure 7-9]. In the final analysis, conservation is not a set of rules, but an attitude—that the living world in all its forms deserves our respect and protection.

BIBLIOGRAPHY

Bohlke, J. E. and C. G. Chaplin. *Fishes of the Bahamas and Adjacent Tropical Waters.* Livingston Publishing Co., Wynnewood, PA, 1968.

Chaplin, C. G. *Fishwatcher's Guide to West Atlantic Coral Reefs* (revised edition). Harrowood Books, Newtown Square, PA, 1972.

Colin, P. *Caribbean Reef Invertebrates and Plants.* T.F.H. Publishing Co., Neptune City, NJ, 1978.

Greenberg, I. and J. Greenberg. *Guide to Corals and Fishes of Florida, the Bahamas, and the Caribbean.* Seahawk Press, Miami, FL, 1977.

Humann, P. *Reef Fish Identification; Reef Creature Identification; Reef Coral Identification.* New World Publications, Jacksonville, FL, 1991–1993.

Kaplan, E. *A Field Guide to Coral Reefs of the Caribbean and Florida.* Houghton Mifflin, Boston, MA, 1982.

Randall, J.E. *Caribbean Reef Fishes.* T.F.H. Publishing Co., Neptune City, NJ, 1983.

Thresher, R. *Reef Fish.* Palmetto Publishing Co., Palmetto, FL, 1980.

Wilson, R. *Watching Fishes: Understanding Coral Reef Fish Behavior.* Pisces Books, a division of Gulf Publishing Co., Houston, TX, 1992.

INDEX